ADVFN Guide: 101 Charts for Trading Success

ZAK MIR

ISBN-13: 978-1908756169 (ADVFN Books)
ISBN-10: 1908756160

ADVFN BOOKS

CONTENTS

INTRODUCTION

What attracted me to charting as a method to success on the stock market nearly 25 years ago was a combination of various factors specific to the 1980s. These included privatisations, yuppies and the song "Money for Nothing." The obsession remained despite things we take for granted today, a lack of a cheap PC, a cheap real-time data feed, and decent content on the Internet. But most of all it was laziness. Charting promised to deliver an at-a-glance way of predicting price action and hence gaining riches. Writing my first book notwithstanding, this lazy characteristic has governed my life, and is expected to do so for what it is left of it. It certainly explains why I only spent six weeks studying economics at the LSE. Although unlike Mick Jagger, doing so has not so far been the springboard to rock 'n' roll immortality.

Executed correctly, charting should be a way of delivering high probability percentage trades/investments that remove the task of having to trawl through company accounts, financial ratios, and interviewing megalomaniac CEOs. This form of technical analysis (as opposed to the fundamental variety I have just described) is at best the only legal form of insider-trading. Indeed, there is nothing quite so satisfying as recommending a stock days before a takeover bid on the basis of its charting configuration alone.

In *101 Charts* years of laziness will be suspended in order to deliver an exhaustive guide to making money via identifying price patterns, trends and signals.

101 Charts is a tricks of the trade publication that will hopefully explain some of the most complex set ups in the market as simply as possible and with no mention of logarithms or algebra, or other techno babble that very often plague "expert" investment/trading magazines. The combination of the analysis here is of trend lines, chart patterns, RSI and as much common sense as can be mustered.

It is inevitable that some of the examples as they are skewed toward the present (and the most difficult market conditions) will date well and some embarrassingly badly. For the latter group we have stop losses and more lessons to learn. But the prediction game is one of nothing ventured, nothing gained, and at least to my mind a sitting on the fence opinion is the worst thing that can be offered in the financial markets.

Oh, and the big reason for reading this book, the three T's. Timing,

Timing, Timing. I don't care if you are Warren Buffet and have never looked at a chart in your life. TA is all about timing and so cannot be ignored.

Even before I begin I would like to address a potential criticism of the format of this book. Hindsight is of course a wonderful thing and therefore it is easy to look smart after an event – say the fall of Lehman Brothers – and boast that it was an obvious eventuality. It was not, that is why it was such a major event and still sends shivers down Wall Street and beyond. But the theory with *101 Charts* is to dissect the build-up to such an event and glean the warning signs for collapses, and the first glimmers in the dark before the big rallies. I would suggest that if you cannot interpret a past event in a constructive manner, when trying to anticipate what will happen at the cold, hard right edge of a chart you will not stand a chance of success.

FINDING OPPORTUNITIES

As well as the hindsight factor, there is the issue of having a lookout system in place. Only after the event is it possible to filter the cream of the crop in terms of the best set ups over a given period. *101 Charts* is a conglomeration of the greatest charting hits over recent generations, as well as the best of the bunch in the recent past. While there is a risk of some of the set ups going stale, there is a skew towards not only the most difficult/surprise moves of the past, but also the most troublesome situations of the recent past. This is on the basis of my view that the markets are like viruses that constantly evolve to be more and more deadly. The assumption in 2011 is that if a trader who is able to make a decent living now went back to say, 1990 he or she would be the George Soros or Warren Buffett of that time if only on the basis that the massive growth in the amount of money moving around the world and the speeding up of this movement via the internet means that volatility is greater than ever.

If you agree with the idea that the markets move in the direction of greatest collective loss, then the search for a secure methodology is something that every trader should be interested in attaining and hopefully this book will point them in the correct direction.

A point of contention that has to arise in terms of providing examples of charting situations of interest is the way that every day on the stock market there are thousands of set ups and let downs waiting to be traded or avoided. How do you find them? Given the way that my day job is writing on Zaks-TA.com where there is a daily stream of stocks in the news, major markets, and highlights from different sectors I am forced to be eagle eyed at all times. But there are limits. Even the most ardent fan of stocks is probably only going to be familiar with the main indices commodities and say 20 or 30 leading stocks. Out of these at any given time it could be the case that only a handful or even less are presenting compelling opportunities.

Therefore we need technology to provide a helping hand. Particularly useful to me is looking at any financial website where the top ten percentage winners and losers are tabled during the day with ADVFN.com leading the way in the online offering. Indeed, stock screening that really makes the difference, with my preferred methods in terms of software being to use Sharescope (www.sharescope.com) for finding the biggest winners and losers of the recent past and Updata's (www.updata.co.uk).

With Sharescope's and Updata's TraderPro software (I have both) you have the ability to identify moving average golden/dead crosses, chart gaps and bearish divergence. Concentrating on mining for just these technical configurations should at least ensure that you are not overwhelmed with potential trading opportunities and can then distil down the best available.

A point that may assure some is the way that of the examples included that were spotted at the time they actually tended to be the more difficult ones rather than the easiest to identify. It could very well be the case that applying the approach of *101 Charts* it is the simplest set ups that you benefit from. Ironically, it is the simplest signals – golden/dead crosses/support or resistance breaks that can be the most difficult to follow as they tend to occur at times when sentiment or logic requires a counter intuitive suspension of belief.

CHARTS IN HISTORY

1. 9/11

A key feature of charting is that trading decisions are made solely on the basis of the price patterns and trends you see in front of you. Ideally, you are taking an objective and dispassionate view on the stock or market that is being analysed, something which even at the best of times can be a very difficult thing to do. There is no greater example of this than the immediate aftermath of the September 11th, 2001 attacks.

For those of my parents' generation, the biggest shared single event of their lives was probably the assassination of President Kennedy. But for those who are now 60 and under, it is 9/11 of which we remember where we were and what we were doing. A decade of geopolitical deterioration has ensued, with little apparent interest in addressing the issues involved. It would appear that the human need to have an enemy is still very much in place, largely because there is money in it, it provides a sense of cultural identity and perhaps most importantly, it is a great booster for political leaders. Of course, alcohol, drugs, junk food and speeding motorists continue to carry a greater mortality than terrorism, or the war against it. But none of these enemies have quite the same cross cultural frisson of opportunity, except maybe the tax raising battle over alleged climate change.

The Set Up

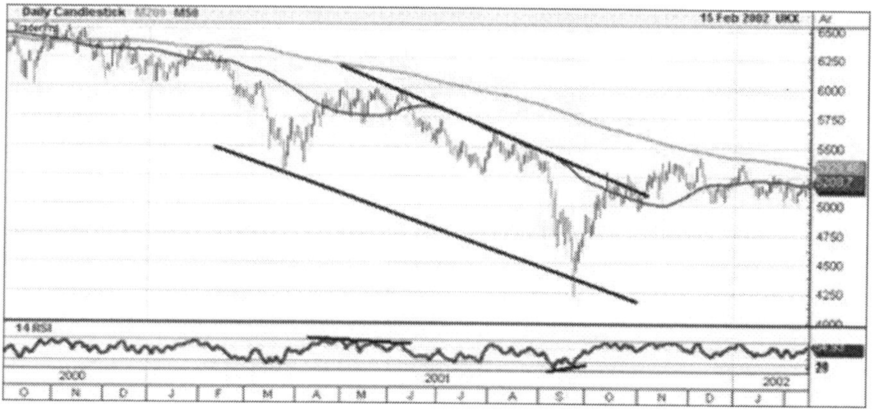

As can be seen from the daily chart of the FTSE 100 for 2001 we were looking at a falling blue chip index going into September, as the unwinding of the dot-com bubble continued for the UK stock market. The seeds of the autumn decline were sown in April/May as bearish divergence was shown in the RSI window, echoing multiple failures at the 6,000 level for the UK index. From August 16th it was possible to draw the line that capped this market going into 9/11, with September 6th witnessing an end of day close below post May 5,200 support. At this point we had a shorting opportunity on the basis of the June resistance line, falling near term moving averages, and the loss of four month support. The floor of the March price channel at 4,250 delivered a one to two month target for the FTSE 100.

Outcome

Conspiracy theorists could argue that equity markets – or at least some participants had an inkling that a terrorist attack was in the offing. But the picture is clouded by the way we were already in bear mode. Usually there is a way of telling whether the market has been genuinely surprised or not. A bolt from the blue shock event (BP (BP.)/Macondo 2010) will deliver an initial low on the day in question – with that support broken as those caught on the hop head for the exit on any initial dead cat bounce. But once these sellers are out – and there is "no one" left to sell, there can very often be a sharp reaction to the upside.

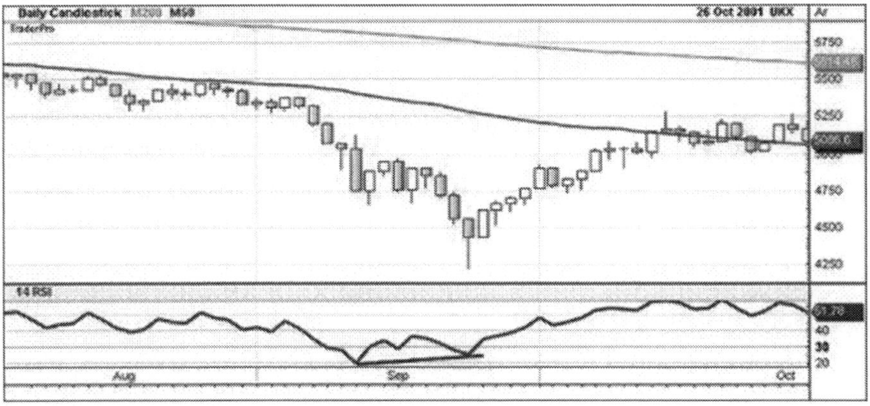

The aftermath of 9/11 essentially followed the bolt from the blue pattern with the FTSE 100 going into a continuation bear flag above 4,700 before a new wave of sellers came in. They fulfilled the March support line projection target of 4,250. But there was more. The September 21st low of 4,219 was over 400 points lower than the September 11th low. However, the RSI on the 11th was 19 and on the 21st 25. This was an instance of massive bullish divergence, a clear buy signal and one that I called at the time. A point to note is that because the Dow was closed between the 10th and the 17th there was no such technical set up, hence the appearance of the FTSE 100 for 9/11.

Conclusion:

The events of 9/11 coincided with a bear phase for equity markets, something which most likely meant that the selling climax which followed caused a sharper rebound in stocks than might have been expected. Nevertheless, a 30% decline from the best levels of 2000 limited the downside.

2. The Baghdad Bounce

The Set Up

Coming less than 18 months after 9/11 and with obvious fundamental linkage, the rally in stocks that accompanied the second Iraq invasion lived up to the famous Rothschild adage of buying to the sound of the first gunfire. These words of wisdom apparently worked very well in the Napoleonic Wars, and turned out to be equally suitable as a kick-off to one of the greatest bull runs ever between 2003 and 2007. If there was a surprise associated with this turnaround it was that at the time the FTSE 100 appeared to have one more leg to the downside and to the 3,000 zone in it.

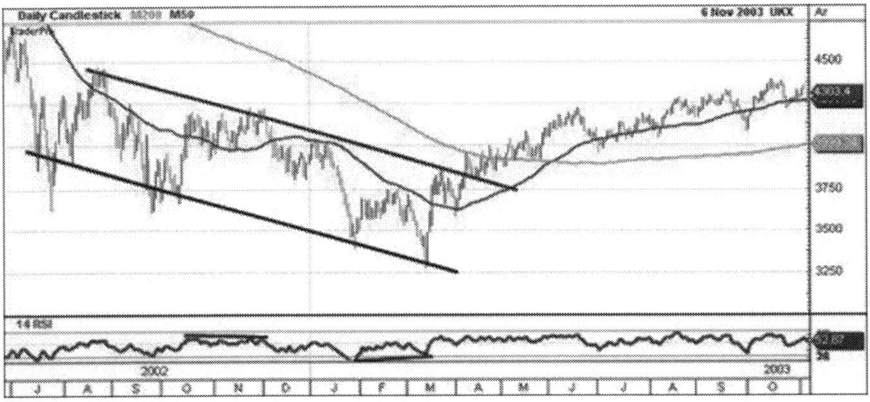

On the daily chart of the FTSE 100 going into the March 2003 turnaround it can be seen how a post June 2002 falling trend channel added to the bearish misery of the price action. The UK index was also well below the red 200 day moving average which is the dividing line between bull and bear modes. On this basis alone there was no reason to blink as far as the bears were concerned unless or until there was a clearance of the price channel top towards 3,800, or the red 200 day line at 3,900. But the problem with waiting on a break of the upper 3,000's zone is that by that time traders would have been nearly 20% off the bottom of the market. In fact, as in the case of 9/11, it was once again the relative strength index which delivered the best long entry signal.

The beginning of the end of the bear phase came on January 29th with a 3,391 low on price and RSI 20. This was an almost direct bounce off the floor of the 2002 price channel and a buy for some 400 points in its own right. However, March 12th delivered a 3,277 low and a 28 RSI – a great bullish divergence signal as well as being another bounce off the 2002 line.

Outcome

Here there was the chance of another 400 plus profit to the price channel top/red 200 day moving average at 3,999, although it has to be admitted that anyone who bought this market for such of the prize may have felt a little compulsion to remain in place much beyond the 200 day line. It was also an example of the stock market proving itself to be as much as 18 months ahead of reality in terms of a recovery in economic fundamentals, and therefore there was little to back the idea of buy and hold up to that point.

Payoff

This was another victory for RSI divergence, which when combined with a trendline rebound is the best way of calling the bottom in a market with a valid stop loss and without the typical white knuckle ride associated with bottom fishing.

3. The Flash Crash

The Set Up

Given the way that the credit crunch and the post credit crunch period have delivered a financial crisis as serious as any of the big economic downturns in 100 years, it has been somewhat surprising that there has been no stock market crash such as 1929 or 1987 to accompany it. And the nearest we managed to get, at least in terms of the name of the event, was the flash crash of May 6th, 2010. Although this occurred during the evening in terms of London time I was actually sitting in front of a screen watching the downfall nearly 10% in just a matter of minutes – an eerie echo of the way indices tumbled on 9/11. In fact my first reaction was to go to the Google news page to see whether some serious fundamental/terror event was taking place. On the day the explanation for the flash crash was no more threatening than fat finger type trade in Procter & Gamble (PG). But the official explanation which came out nearly five months later on September 30th from the SEC pointed to a hedge in the E Mini S&P taken by a mutual fund being undermined by day traders selling off the back of the 75,000 contract sell program.

The first point to note is how clumsy the initial hedging move was, the second what jackals short-term traders are in the market, and the third how it took five months before the powers that be managed to work out what happened. In the meantime there could have been a flash crash every week.

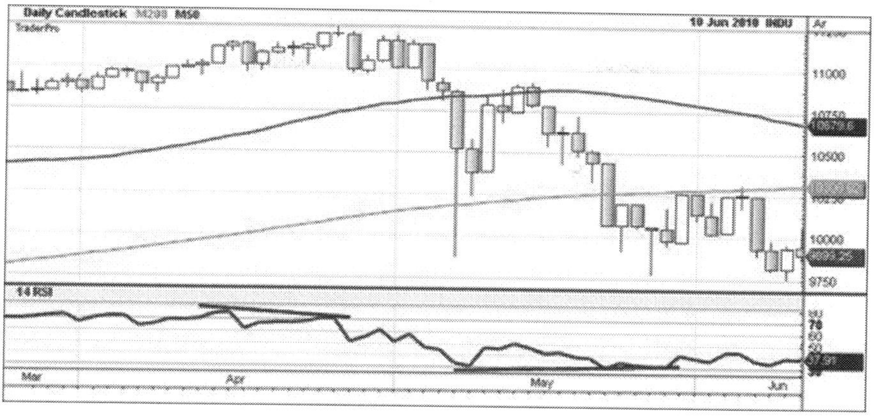

Outcome

It is perhaps just as well that from the perspective of *101 Charts* the fundamental reasons/causes of the flash crash are less relevant than the price action itself. The technical perspective centres around this event being yet another example of the market moving in the direction of greatest collective financial loss, as well as a rather extreme search for support in what was already a very jittery market. Looking at the daily chart of the first nine months of 2010, it can be seen how the traditional early January sell-off delivered a low in the 9,800 zone. This became the focus of support for the first nine months of the year with the flash crash being the first major test. That it would have happened anyway albeit in a slower manner is confirmed by the way that there were three clear tests of the region starting at the end of May, June and July. Even this was not enough. August delivered a final bear trap low below 10,000, one that signalled the start of an autumn rally at which the September component was the best scene in that month for 71 years.

Put in the anthropomorphic way which can be very useful as an aid to understanding, the flash crash was the first and most ambitious attempt by the Dow to make sure that the bulls of this market did not remain in place to enjoy that once-in-a-lifetime September rally. If this concept seems cruel or evil, that is exactly what it is. Making easy money is not supposed to be an easy process. Ironically, this rule was not strictly true on this occasion as technical traders are likely to have been short going into the May 6th debacle. This is said on the basis of the bearish divergence in the RSI window between the two major April highs on the Dow, and by the way near term 11,000 support had already been lost by May 4th. Indeed, it may well have been that the reason for the sharp rebound on May 6th was the frantic short-covering of those who had enjoyed a windfall in the wake of the freak event occurring.

Payoff

The end of August 2010 was a very interesting time in the equity markets, and one I remember with great satisfaction. Those following the financial media would have read headlines such as the death of equities, a technical sell signal known as the Hindenburg omen, and the forecast from an analyst at the leading French investment house suggesting a bloodbath was imminent. For those following the Dow a rather simple message from the daily chart was that support was coming in just below the 10,000 level, and that any weakness towards this area could be regarded as a buying opportunity. My view was that the fundamental bears were getting desperate – even throwing in the technical mumbo-jumbo of Hindenburg.

At the time of writing in December 2010 the year so far for the Dow Jones has delivered no less than seven tests of the 10,000 area. While there may be some calamitous event, worse than any Eurozone failure or terror strike, enough has been done to my mind to ensure that this market is heading north in any substantial way and for a significant period of time. In other words, I'm not backing the idea of eighth time unlucky.

4. The Fall Of Lehman Brothers

The Set Up

As if to underline the area of the destructive nature of the financial markets from the start of the credit crunch in August 2007, a lack of lending between financial institutions meant that one by one the weakest would start to asphyxiate. In effect, there was a domino effect in place as to which major name would be the first to fall. In the UK it was September 14th, 2007 when Northern Rock asked the Bank of England for a bailout. But the real action was to follow on nearly a year to the day later with Northern Rock being the first bank to fail since the middle of the Victorian era.

On September 15th, 2009 the unthinkable happened to a much bigger fish than Northern Rock – Lehman Brothers filed for bankruptcy to the tune of $600m. Putting to one side what the financial media said at the time and since, I have two unchangeable views regarding this incident. The first is that Lehman could not have reached a state of affairs without a little help from friends on Wall Street, and that it could have been any of its rivals that fell alongside it. This is of course no great revelation, it is just common sense. The relevance to this episode as far as one and one charts is concerned is that it provides a very good compare and contrast between the feeling at the time that this event marked a fundamental point, and the way that there were still another six months to go before the stock market hit the bottom.

Outcome

From a charting perspective the summer of 2008 exhibited weak to very weak price action with resistance on the Dow coming in at or below late 2008 support in the 11,800 to 12,000 zone. If only on this basis the US stock average was a sell into strength, especially as rumours of dark events to come on Wall Street were rife over the quiet news flow days of summer. In the end we were treated to a triple whammy consisting of Lehman's Chapter 11, Merrill Lynch selling itself to Bank of America (BAC) and the AIG bailout. It could be argued that while Lehman/Merrill Lynch were positives, the massive bailout of "too big to fail" AIG was what ensured that there would be a further six months of bear market for equities.

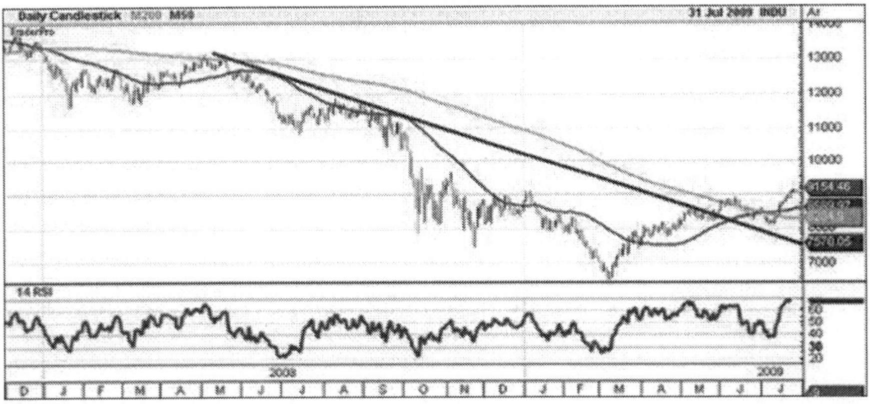

Following the fall of Lehman there were three new lower lows for the Dow Jones. I have to admit that since the 2003 Baghdad Bounce every March has become a potential rallying period. It was therefore not too much of a surprise when bullish divergence led to turn around in the US stock average and a rather irrational (at the time) rally started. The trick however in this instance was that there was such a delay (six months) between the fundamental events reaching rock bottom and the stock market flagging the start of potential economic recovery. Indeed, if the trajectory of the falling 2008 falling price channel is observed, it can be seen how one might have been forgiven for thinking that leading US stocks were due for a strike of the 6,000 area before recovery might set in. Even 18 months later the post Credit Crunch recovery leaves many in the market scratching their heads.

Payoff

Those with deep pockets would have been buying shares for the long haul from September 2008 onwards, if only on the basis that the collapse of major financial institutions had to mark a fundamental, psychological and technical floor. Clearly it would have been a rocky ride, but the Dow at some 8,000 versus 11,000 a couple of years later was a decent and believable eventuality. From a technical perspective this was one of the messier series in stock market history and the charts certainly reflected this confusion. The fall in July 2008 price channel was finally broken in terms of its resistance line of 8,000 at the end of April 2009. This was a robust buy signal, especially as by that time the 50 day moving average could act as a reliable trailing stop loss.

5. The Wall Street Crash of 1929

Even though the Crash of 1929 is now a lifetime away, it remains the benchmark for all financial market disasters, and justifiably so. My knowledge of the era begins and ends with the Charleston, Flappers, the Great Gatsby, and Prohibition. Therefore, I will not indulge in any potted history of the era other to point out what I heard recently, that more millionaires were created during the Great Depression than at any other time in US history. As those buying commodities stocks have found since the Credit Crunch began, there are ways of turning disasters into opportunity.

The Set Up

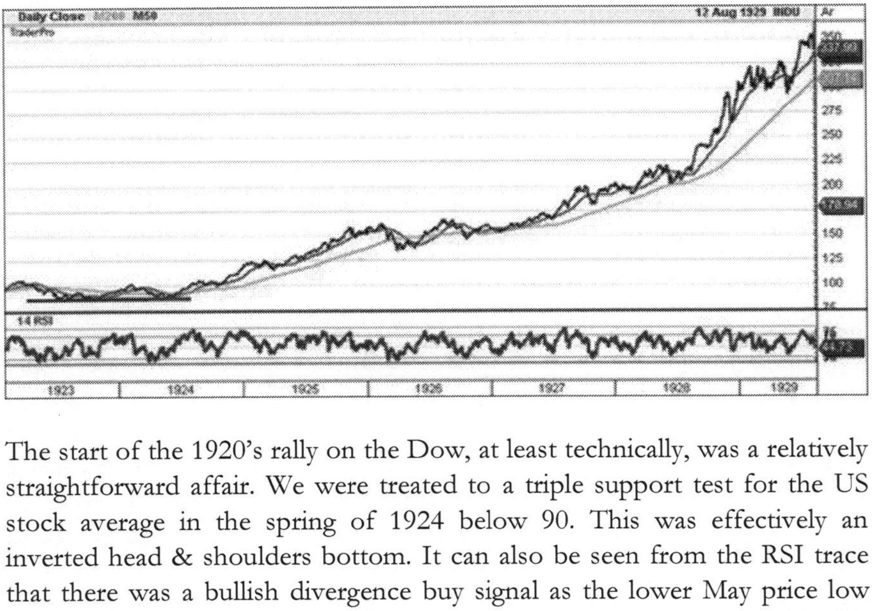

The start of the 1920's rally on the Dow, at least technically, was a relatively straightforward affair. We were treated to a triple support test for the US stock average in the spring of 1924 below 90. This was effectively an inverted head & shoulders bottom. It can also be seen from the RSI trace that there was a bullish divergence buy signal as the lower May price low was not matched by a dip for the oscillator. The major catch with this indicator is that it was not invented until 1978 by Welles Wilder and therefore only Dr Who or the crew of Star Trek could have gone back in time to avail themselves of this method of trading. Nevertheless, we can at least learn from this past example for future reference. The early bird bull signals were followed by a golden cross between the 50/200 day moving averages. This would provide an entry point at the end of July at around the 100 points mark. Those awaiting further confirmation that the good times were about to roll could have waited on the higher October low above the 200 day moving average then in the low 90s, plus the break of a bull flag pattern at 105 shortly after.

There was then a clear 50% gain for the Dow to be riding on until the 200 day moving average was lost in April 1926. The retreat here was back towards 135 before a new long entry at the end of July at no worse than 165. From this point there was a clear run higher using the 200 day line as a trailing stop loss to the September 1929 381 peak.

I suppose the definition of a Crash is that it is an event which catches out as many people as possible. The way to do this (or more precisely, the way it happens) is via a V shaped turnaround as a low and an A shaped reversal at the top. On anything other than a close view – say six month or shorter period chart, the 381 September 3rd peak simply appears as a straight up/straight down move. On this basis the first warning that anything was awry came from the loss of the 50 day moving average on September 24th, followed by the October 21st close below the 200 day moving average at 321. There was a final test of the 200 day line as new resistance on October 22nd at 327.

A lopsided head & shoulders neckline from July has been drawn down to 310, which would have given you a 305 short entry on October 23rd, but really the most objective and easy to follow signal comes from the interaction between the price and the way a market obtains support and resistance at the key moving averages. But overall I would have to say that this was a market that turned on a dime, especially with relation to the size of the downside which was eventually delivered. Normally you would expect a more extended turnaround. For those who are concerned that an exit of 321 was not too hot as compared to a 381 high, the reason for hanging on here was the sharp October 3rd rebound off the 200 day line – a strong continuation signal. In my opinion 350 on a 50 day moving average failure on October was something even Rockefeller would have been proud of.

Outcome

I have broken up the analysis of the Crash into the time before and after the late October plunge. From October 25th to November 12th this market lost 100 points or a third of its value. This was cruel, but not yet the stuff of legend. This arguably came in the months and years to follow.

If the decline through October was swift, the rebound from the November 200 low was G force inducing, in that it was a manoeuvre giving the impression that the plunge of the autumn had been an aberration and that we were looking at a great bargain hunting opportunity. The fact that by April 1930 leading US stocks were up nearly 50% from the November low may have provided decent vindication of such a theory. However, from this point on the chartists did have a rather more decent armoury than before the Crash began. Resistance for the Dow in April 1930 came in at or below the old early 1929 support, and we would have been looking for a weekly close above the 200 day moving average at 300 to confirm that this market was not a sell into strength. This was underlined by the way that in the wake of the November low we had been treated to a 50/200 day moving average dead cross. Indeed, using the 200 day line alone one's stance on the Dow as being in a sell trend could have sufficed from October 1929 to August 1932 when the line was finally broken to the upside. This period included the low of the bear market at 41 on July 8th 1932.

But I have saved the worst until last. This came on October 10th 1930 when the previous year's 200 low was broken. This delivered the start of a second Crash which lasted until the aforementioned summer 1932 low point. Such a move in the present day would see the lows of 2009 revisited in 2011/2012 after a failure for the Dow at 11,000 (it fell from 14,000 to under 7,000 in 2007-9). So far we have bounced higher than the 1930 peak – the equivalent of 315 versus 299, although it may pay to be cautious just a little longer.

Payoff

Even with the benefit of 80 plus years of hindsight there is not much to go on in terms of where a 1920s investor would have run for the hills on a technical basis. A 2010s investor would have the RSI indicator which could have warned from August of bearish divergence in the RSI window, and perhaps this would have provided an opportunity to take profits in September at over 350. But the possibility of being hurt in the wake of a re-entry to the early October 200 day moving average rebound always remained.

To my mind there was enough cruelty and pain inflicted by the price action of the Dow in the run up to and aftermath of the Crash of '29, that we have more than enough of an explanation as to the causes of the Great Depression, the fight between communism and capitalism, as well as the inspiration for WWII. It may also provide the explanation as to why ever since, when the going gets tough Governments would rather go bust than risk civil unrest. Hence, the squeeze since then has been on the middle classes, who in general do not run amok even if they have no money to pay for college fees, shopping at Waitrose or having the Land Rover serviced.

FT 30 1973-1974 The Oil Crisis

e I came in as far as interest in the financial markets was con... Every morning on the way to school the London news station LBC broadcast the stock market report, and I listened. Perhaps not many other seven year olds like our Dave (Prime Minister David Cameron is just a few weeks younger than me) were gripped by where the stock market was going. However, I was, and this may explain why I am not Prime Minister. After the stock prices and the level of the FT 30 – always falling – came Bob Beckman, a feisty New York investment guru (the founder of the Investors' Bulletin) who provided some Stateside glamour to grey London autumn mornings. At the time in 1973 I knew nothing of what an investment banker or stockbroker did, or the ups and downs that Beckman had already been through and the way that like anyone else, some of his calls did not always go the right way. Nevertheless, the seeds were sown as far as the idea of being a financial markets guru, or at least daring to predict where they are going,

In fact, what I remember of Beckman at the time is that he kept on insisting that even though UK stocks were falling like a stone, there would be a mighty recovery. From what I know now shares were falling so fast and so low that there had to be a dead cat bounce in the wake of the economic woes of the early 1970s. However, it was not actually a done deal. If, as was thought at the time by some, the UK risked falling to communism (an amazing thought) the FT 30 would have been dead in the water.

The Set Up

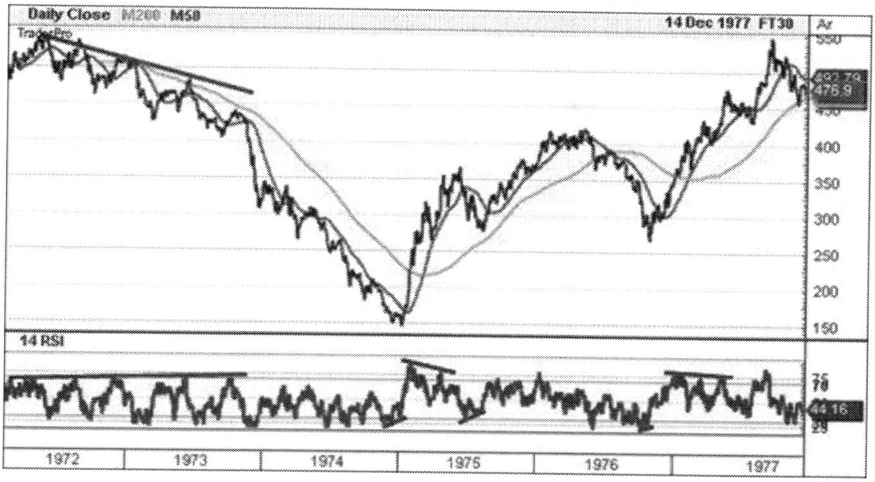

The rather irritating Credit Crunch phrase "perfect storm" found its real scenario in the early 1970s: a falling US Dollar, the Middle East a hotbed of enmity, and a surprisingly united (as compared to now) Arab/Islamic alliance. On October 17th 1973 in the wake of the Yom Kippur war OPEC raised the price of Crude Oil by nearly three quarters. I would presume that the effect of these events plus the end of Bretton Woods in 1971 (convertibility of Gold to the US Dollar) plus Vietnam plus having Richard "Tricky Dicky" Nixon as US President must have made the events after the Credit Crunch on Wall Street seem like a tea party.

The UK may not have been communist, but the power of the unions would probably have made the Kremlin jealous. Their power in business prevention/anti wealth creation knew no equal until the arrival of the Quangos/the FSA and EU decades later. It is also evident that the plight of the economy in 2010 has many similarities with that of 1975 – the last time we had a Coalition Government (comedy show). It will be interesting to see whether George Osborne will win the Denis Healey Award for best executed trip to the IMF.

Outcome

The result of all the pain of the early 1970s was that UK shares fell by over 75% from their August 1972 peak to the worst levels at the start of 1975. Perhaps the worst aspect of this was that the good times, in the UK the

"Barber Boom", had not actually been that fantastic in terms of fat stored up for the lean times. Like the run up to the 2007-2008 banking bust there had been lax lending on an overheating housing market, with a resultant bailout of secondary banks by the Bank of England. The problem in this country is that we were already in the midst of this crisis when the oil price hike struck. I suppose the equivalent today (2010) to the OPEC action would be if for some reason mortgage rates had to double overnight when most consumers are already on the edge after two years of retrenchment.

From a charting perspective the intro to the October 1973 bombshell was a rather curious mix. Lower highs and lows meant that the bulls would have at the very least been running to stand still, although long term investors might not have thought there was anything untoward going on.

The technical configuration of a falling channel and falling moving averages going into autumn 1973 meant that the easiest way forward here would have been short, and would have been to do so on any strength towards the 200 day moving average. It helped that the spring of that year had already delivered a 50/200 day moving average dead cross close to the 500 mark. Given that the low was an uninterrupted move down to 150 from the signal one could say that this was one of the best bear indicators ever.

As in the case of the Wall Street Crash it feels somewhat inappropriate to call upon the RSI indicator given that it was still five years away from being invented. But there were multiple oscillator failures going into late 1973.

A highlight of the move down once it started is that new resistance through 1974 came in at or even below former support. This is something witnessed in the worst of situations – which this period can safely be described as being. The twist (and there almost is one) was the turnaround. There was little charting warning. True, the bear trap back above 150 helped, as did the break back above the 50 day moving average in the 160's, but without the help of the bullish divergence from the RSI the rebound was a V shaped/turning on a dime affair. Only well into 1975 and well above the 200 day moving average at 230 plus was really enough to signal the worst was over.

Rather unhelpfully the recovery after the initial V bounce was a three steps forward/two steps back affair – witnessed by the way 1973 support become 1976 resistance and a bear trap below the mid-1975 support. This was a bear market that firstly did not want to quit, and second did not want anyone who had bought low to have an easy ride.

Payoff

The impression given by the FT 30 trace going into the 1974 nightmare is that even as late as early autumn the year before we were going into a relatively soft downturn. I would suspect that for those actually involved in trading stocks at this time it was the bottom fishers who took as much pain as those who had simply been caught out by just another boom/bust. "Modern" markets tend to see the worst price hit at the time of, or just after (once bottom fishers have been stopped out). It would appear that somehow these days there are very few genuine shock events. In this case the OPEC move caused the FT 30 to halve, suggesting genuine surprise and worry. This probably delivered around 100 points of overshoot on what the real low should have been, 250-300, rather than 150 – hence the V shaped rebound and the way that support did come in between 250-300 in 1975-1977. If you were on the ball you would have spotted the break of a 1974 falling wedge pattern/50 day moving average break at the end of January 1975 to go long of the FT 30 at 170. Unfortunately, I was wasting time at school. RSI bullish divergence which could have found the big buying opportunity had not been invented – there was a great oscillator buy signal here, but one that was only on offer to time travellers.

7. The 1987 Stock Market Crash

The Set Up

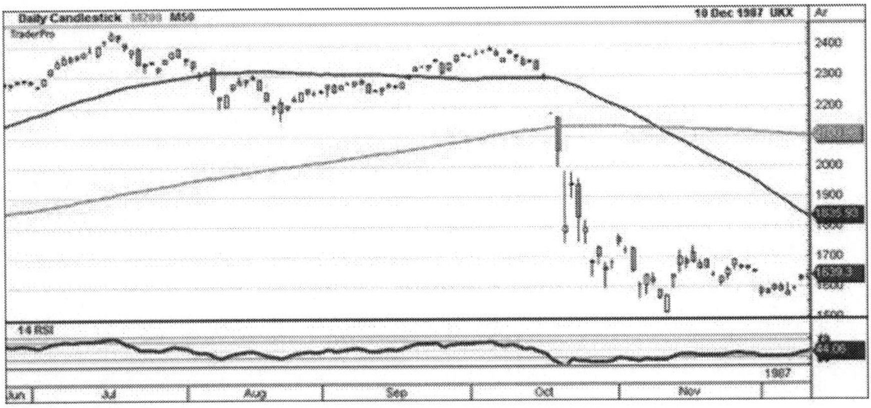

For some reason the markets of yesteryear always appear to be a walk in the park as compared to what is going on now. This even applies to the events prior to and immediately after the stock market Crash of 1987. Indeed this major rug pulling event now has the aspect of being rather less difficult to handle than the Flash crash of 2010, which has already almost been forgotten.

Even so we cannot help but be impressed on hearing anecdotal evidence of smart players of the 1980s such as James Goldsmith who headed for the exit with their profits well before the Crash of '87 struck. Presumably Sir James had spotted the typical asset bubble characteristics of the mid-1980s period, just as obvious to him as the oversized mobile phones and yuppies are to us now in pictures of the period. Privatisations in the UK, as the Thatcher government moved to sell off the family silver, were extremely popular, but also underlined that in this country at least there was no one left to push share prices higher.

Outcome

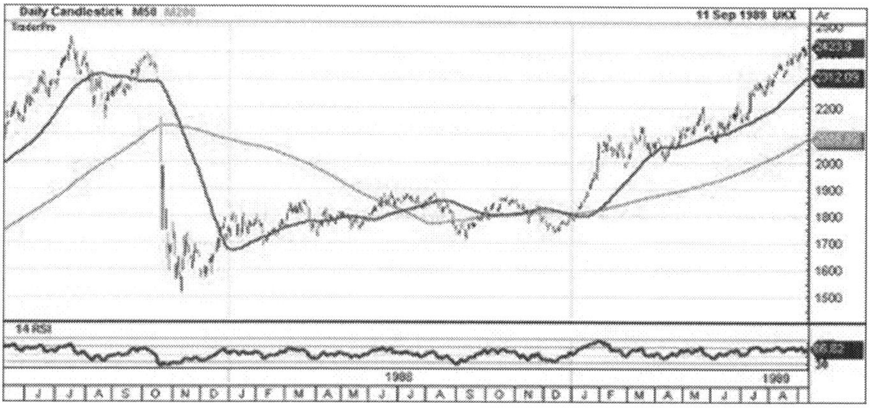

Given the way that the Crash of '87 was the inspiration for my entry into this particular vocation, it may be imagined that I have looked at the price action preceding the collapse on several occasions. Rather unhelpfully as far as those attempting to hone in their predictive skills, and flattering those who manage to exit their portfolios before October 19th, it can be said that the degree of difficulty at least on a technical basis is very high year. While the magnitude of any move following a signal can be difficult to ascertain even at the best of times, the post-April triangle could just as easily have been a continuation feature ahead of a new leg up through 2,400 on the FTSE 100. In fact, it was the weekly close below the 50 day moving average/April support line at 2,300 ahead of Black Monday which remains the best and easiest to sell signal to remember for future melt downs. Of course once this trigger had been activated a measured move 500 point fall based on the left side of the post-April triangle, and the idea of a retest of April support near 1,900 kicked into play.

Nevertheless, I maintain that the '87 plunge was as difficult to avoid if you were long as it was to short if you were a bear. This is even if you were certain that the triple failure at 2,400 would be as damaging as it turned out to be. Such events always tend to leave market participants as stunned rabbits in the headlights, with most either missing out as they wait for the right moment to enter, and of course those with their holdings in the market hoping for the storm to pass without decimating their holdings.

Payoff

It is understandable that in the years that followed the 1987 crash, it became the benchmark for any violent decline in equity values. It may very well be that even though we've had several valid reasons to crash in a similar fashion since then, the memory of this decline acts as a deterrent. Therefore the chances of it happening in quite the same way, at least while there are people in the market old enough to remember the event, are relatively slim. In fact, the main positive message to take away from late 1987 is the way that we were treated to a relatively clean break down/recovery and that those who decided to bottom fish (off the back of bullish RSI divergence) in late October and early November where never really challenged by further adverse price action.

8. ERM Exit September 16th 1992

The Set Up

The UK has always been a semi-detached member of Europe, and perhaps this is the way it should always and will always be. The events of 1992 going into Sterling's eviction from the Exchange Rate Mechanism, a dry run for what was to become the Euro, underlined how we currently have, and have always had the worst of both worlds in terms of the relationship with Europe. Taxpayers' cash is delivered to Brussels as if we were a first tier member but because of the lack of currency union when the UK banks went bust the ECB could just look on and laugh given its lack of liability.

Now as the EU unravels we can look on and laugh, albeit after not being able to join the single currency courtesy of philanthropist/hedge fund owner George Soros. It is ironic that if the UK had been in with the big boys, France and Germany, many of the problems the entity faces may have been avoided. My view, a cynical one, is that the economic position of the US was undermined (if only as the Euro being an alternative "reserve" currency) from the day it came into being at the beginning of the last decade, and that we are in a situation in which either the US/US Dollar collapses or the Single Currency disintegrates.

The best scenario and perhaps the less painful one is ironically an indefinite Mexican standoff of near zero interest rates and competitive devaluation. In the meantime S&P/Fitch/Moody's trash PIIGS nations' credit ratings and not that of the US whenever a run on the Dollar is threatened. As we didn't join the Eurozone, the UK is seemingly rewarded by a AAA rating, although given the state of the nation's debt and in the wake of the banking collapse one wonders under what nightmare scenario this might ever be lost.

As far as Sterling is concerned the privilege of the Bank of England being able to generate stagflation and save the likes of HBOS, Northern Rock, and RBS is not one that I would have fought for. But of course, no UK Prime Minister would want to be labelled the one who got rid of the Pound and a lost a fistful of banks – even Mrs Thatcher had enough problems cutting off milk to school children – as a milk snatcher in the 1970s.

Outcome

I have little doubt that the Coalition Government will eventually make the John Major Government appear as something akin to President Kennedy's Camelot. But going into September 1992 we were treated to a comedy of errors in order to keep the UK in the ERM including raising interest rates to 15% - if only very temporarily. It was certainly embarrassing, but if you look at it most post war administrations have had to eat humble pie, except Margaret Thatcher – although even she was forcibly evicted from Number 10 in 1990.

Perhaps what was lucky as far as the trajectory of the FTSE 100 was concerned going into Sterling's big eviction is that the UK index was already coming off the back of a severe recession (yes, another one). This is shown on the weekly chart by the 1990 and 1992 bounces off the 200 week moving average on the weekly chart. A plus for the FTSE 100 was that the shadow of the 1987 Crash remained, which meant that an event would have to be extremely negative to impact on the recovery mode. There was also the rather obvious point that most in the City and elsewhere regarded anything to do with the EU/ERM/foreigners (if they cared or understood at all) as simply something to be avoided at all costs, so the reaction to the exit was a very positive one.

This can be seen on the daily chart close up in terms of the sharp bear trap on the day below the 2,300 level, and then the gap higher on September 17th. This gapping action in cross proximity to the 200 day moving average – already rising – could only have been regarded as bullish. Those who were not that convinced could have waited either for October's double gap to the upside above the 200 day moving average, and November's 50/200 day moving average, both suitable flags to one of the greatest decades for the stock market – the 1990s.

Payoff

While the implications of the UK's exit from the ERM could be argued about for years, both in terms of the benefits to the UK or the damage to the EU, the episode is a good example of how in many ways it is difficult to keep a good trend down. While there was the volatility on the day and immediately after the event, essentially the FTSE 100 was already on its way in terms of mega bull run whose roots had developed in the wake of the 1987 Crash.

9. Bank of England Gets Its "Independence" May 6th 1997

The Set Up

Given the £800bn debt the UK was weighed under by mid-2010, and the chronic target beating inflation numbers, the idea of giving independence to the Bank of England in 1997 seemed to be on a par with selling the UK's Gold Reserves formulated soon after in terms of good ideas. But it was a New Government/New Labour and actually an idea which in theory at least seemed to be sensible.

In particular it would seemingly break the tradition of the financial markets regarding Labour fiscal policy with suspicion. This way, if things now went badly the Government could blame The Bank and if they went well it could take the credit itself. As things turned out, there was no more independence possible between The Treasury and The Bank of England than between Tweedledee and Tweedledum. In addition, the ultimate responsibility lies with the Chancellor/Government, and therefore the Governor of the Bank of England has to spend most of his tenure either avoiding being a fall guy and or avoiding looking like he is passing the buck when something goes wrong.

The Outcome

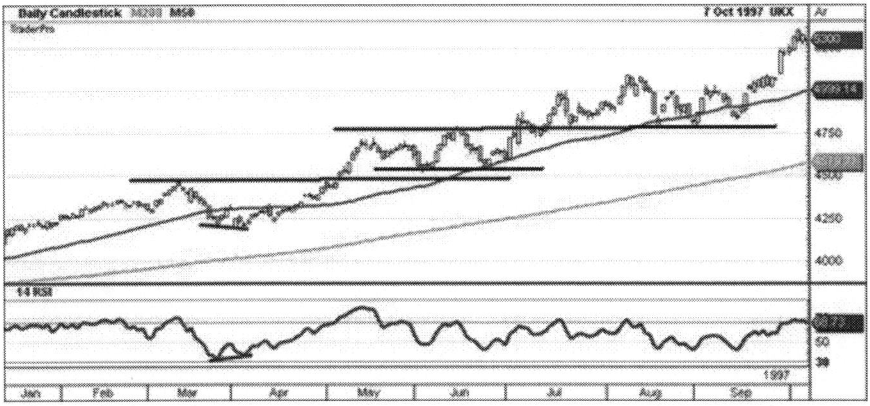

I remember the sea of blue on the monitor of FTSE 100 stocks as the move to grant the Bank of England independence. Given the weekly chart and the mature bull market the UK index was in by the late 1990s, abolishing the Bank of England or the Treasury would have been greeted in the same bullish fashion. The technical backing for this comes from the way that either side of the May 6th announcement the UK index was building new support at or above former resistance. This is not a common occurrence and is worth savouring, especially when we look back at the "lost decade" for equities between 2000-2009.

The trigger for the bullishness going into May came from bullish RSI divergence at the start of April, with the manifestation being a gap to the upside for the UK index just above the 50 day moving average – essentially an indication of the strength of the latest leg of an extended uptrend. There would be three more gaps to the upside going up to the beginning of August. As well as the phenomenon of old resistance becoming new support, the massive distance between the price action trace and the 200 day moving average underlined how strong this market was over mid-1997 and that almost any event would be interpreted positively, a rather alien state of affairs after what we have been through since the Credit Crunch.

Payoff

As well as being a walk down memory lane at one of the more significant events as far as the UK financial markets were concerned in recent years, revisiting the sweet spot of the 1990s bull run is quite an eye opener, particularly as this period appears to be a walk in the park from a charting and/or trading perspective.

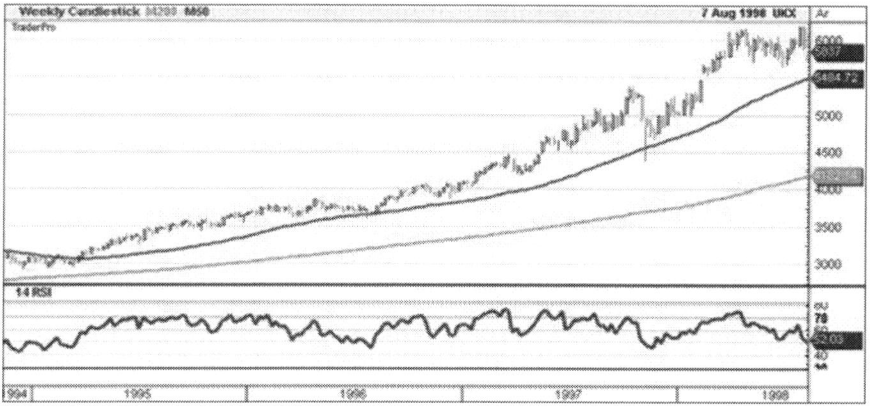

10. The Nikkei 1990

The Set Up

Three years before the fall of Nikkei in 1990 (and the 1987 Crash) I had an argument with an Oxford don on the influence of the Japanese economy over the rest of the world. My argument was that there would only be a recession in Western economies if growth in Japan failed as it was effectively propping them up. His view was that it was a growth economy that would keep on growing (like our BRIC nations today), so we had nothing to fear.

In fact, he probably didn't care but was just trying to keep the conversation going in order to test his latest candidate. Obviously, I failed the interview, going on to achieve the same result for Cambridge and Harvard via a carefully honed Asperger's Syndrome technique.

But I suppose that the ghost of the Oxford don and myself could continue the same argument 25 years later, substituting China for Japan. Perhaps of rather more interest is the way that while many of the historical events echoed in the charts have faded, the crash of the Nikkei is still an ongoing/work in progress situation. If the markets are supposed to flag for coming events in the real world this was the mother of all signals. Indeed, if it is the case Western economies go into a similar double decade stagnation, it could be said justifiably that it all started here in Japan.

Outcome

While it made it possible for some to scratch their heads regarding the setup offered by the chart of the FTSE 100 in 1987, with the Japanese stock market in 1990 the technical house of cards was brought down by the simple break up the trend lines in place since the beginning of 1988. The loss of this line at 37,000 was so swift, as indeed was the loss of the 200 day moving average just above 35,000 shortly after, that there was little opportunity for even the most conscientious bull of Japanese stocks to try their hand at a little falling knife catching. Indeed the first chance to buy the dip came at the 27,000 mark – the first of umpteen false dawn bear market endings from the land of the rising sun. At least up to the end of 1990 a giveaway that the worst was still to come derived from the way that there was such a distance between the price action and the 200 day moving average still falling like a stone.

Payoff

As we shall see from the bursting of the dot-com bubble, there is a relationship between severity of the charging breakdown in the market and the length of the bear market to follow. In the case of the Nikkei had been treated to a 20 year nightmare, it works by periodically delivering egg on face to financial journalists and fund managers calling the bottom prematurely. Presumably when the bull market returns there will be a similarly dramatic/clear-cut set up to get those who have been so patient on board.

11. The Shanghai Surprise October 2007 – Nikkei Mark II?

I have to admit that China being the world's second economy (it really should be classed as number one, given that it is rather more solvent than the US) caught me off guard. When the possibility of it being a great emerging market first came through at the start of the 1990s (1985 if you count the visit of Wham!) it could have been the case that the former communist nation's record on human rights would mean that the West simply would not do business. This was extremely naive thinking as human rights only apply to nations where the US and the allies could successfully engage in military conflict. Currently this would include Burundi, Andorra and San Marino, but it is the principle that counts.

The reasons for the inclusion of the Shanghai Composite are of course firstly as a play on China, second as a compare and contrast with Japan's 1990 peak and third after reading that this market is a leading indicator on the S&P 500.

The Set Up

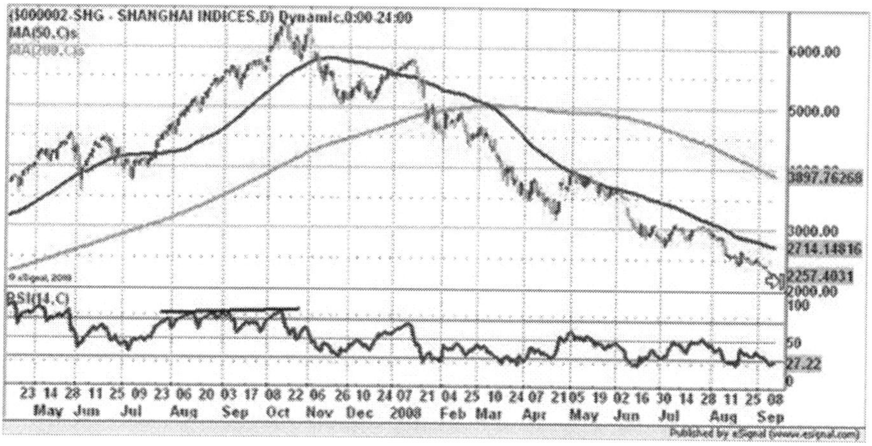

Given all the hope and hype of China as the 21st century victor, for the composite index to rally fivefold in three years seems in order. It also provided a great set up for a bubble. What is evident on the daily chart for much of the journey to the upside is how far above the 200 day moving average it managed to remain for so long. While this may have lulled the bulls into a false sense of security, at least there were decent warnings that positive momentum was being lost.

The big plus here is the appearance of chart gaps from the start of autumn 2007. This process was started at the end of September with two unfilled gaps to the upside. On the face of it we were being treated to a renewed show of strength by this market. Nevertheless, the message was to see how the subsequent price action behaved around these gaps.

Outcome

Initially in October 2007 the Shanghai Composite embraced the late September gaps up with the bottom of the September 28th gap providing a level to buy into on October 26th for a last hurrah rally and October triple top through 6,200. From this point on the alarm bells were ringing loud and clear. The start of November delivered two unfilled gaps to the downside with the November 8th end of day close below October neckline support signalling a major top could be on its way. From this point on only a weekly close back above the second November gap at 6,000 would really have been enough to shake the nerves of the bears. Not that they were put under much pressure. January 2008 brought another neckline failure plus two gaps down from 5,800 again, with little to upset the sellers until March 2009 when the 200 day moving average was crossed at 2,300. Since then the best this market has been able to do is 2,500-3,500.

Payoff

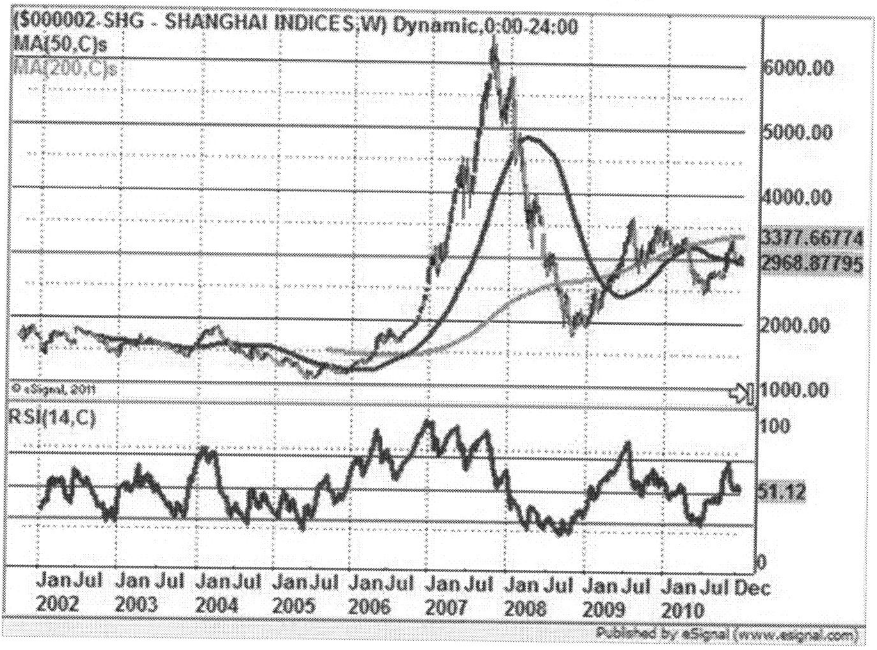

Having essentially sidelined the Chinese economic miracle for what are clearly puerile reasons, I have been surprised that the Shanghai benchmark remains in consolidation mode at best. While it may be too early to suggest that we can rule out a Nikkei style extended slide – this is unthinkable to most intelligent observers – it can be said that the top formed was a very deliberate one, and at least from a charting perspective is likely to weigh heavily for years rather than months.

12. The Dot-com Bubble Bursts

The Set Up

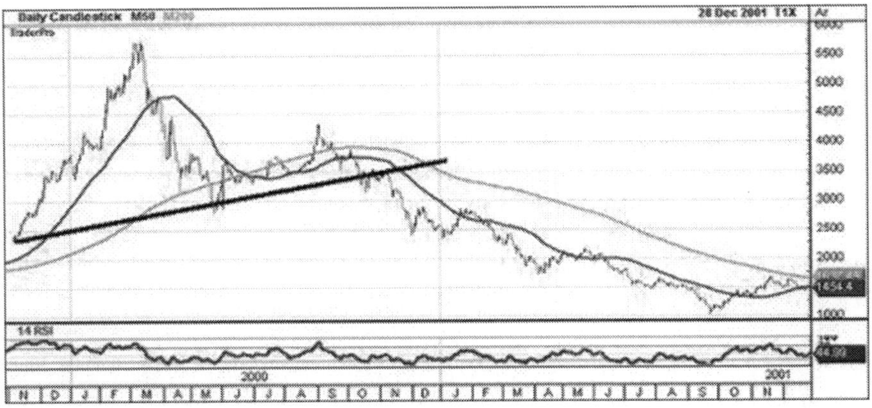

I have to confess that it is only in the past five years or so (since Apple (AAPL) remodelled itself) that I have become a tech/gadget freak. This means that I had the skill to avoid the bust of dot-com bubble on the basis that I was never involved in the first place. It may very well be the same privilege is reserved for me with regard to the current commodities boom. Certainly, the late 1990s going into the millennium, with its attendant bug, represented a time of frenzy with regard to the possibilities of the Internet, computers and technology of all varieties. In many ways this hysteria was justified, it was just a decade too early. Unfortunately in the markets, as many have found out, you lose just as much from being too early as from being too late.

Outcome

It did not help chartists that the near vertical rise and fall for the TechMark 100 in 1999/2000 came before any significant historical data. But even without the presence of mind to draw support line from the autumn of 1999 to the autumn of 2000 through 3,400 as a neckline to be broken, the 2,800 zone emerges as key. This was the first support after the 2000 peak was put in, and became resistance to end 2000, and at the beginning of 2001. Considering that the market was flirting with the 1,000 by the end of the year to exit techs in the upper 2,000's in early 2001 would not have provided any shame for fans of this sector. Indeed, by the end of 2001 it became clear that only sustained price action above the 200 day moving average then above 1,850, would be enough to kill the sell trend in this part of the market.

Payoff

At least to my eyes, the topping out of leading UK technology stocks at the beginning of 2000 is a very similar process to that of the peak in the Japanese stock market almost exactly ten years before. Indeed, the single sharp peak followed by a 30%-50% retracement, and then a drift can be regarded as one of the worst technical set ups to befall any market. Indeed, bulls of technology stocks can count themselves lucky that the TechMark 100 recovered within just a few years, rather than the 20 years and counting we are witnessing on the Nikkei.

13. Dot-com Bubble Case Study: ARM Holdings (ARM): Before the Bubble

Chip designer ARM Holdings is the closest that the UK has to a glamorous tech stock, (supplying Apple (AAPL)) and at least from my perspective had its "barmy army" of fans well before many might imagine what use its products would have. But the geeks were well on board here going into the Dot-com bubble of 1999/2000 and it is well worth looking at the shares during those heady days.

The Set Up

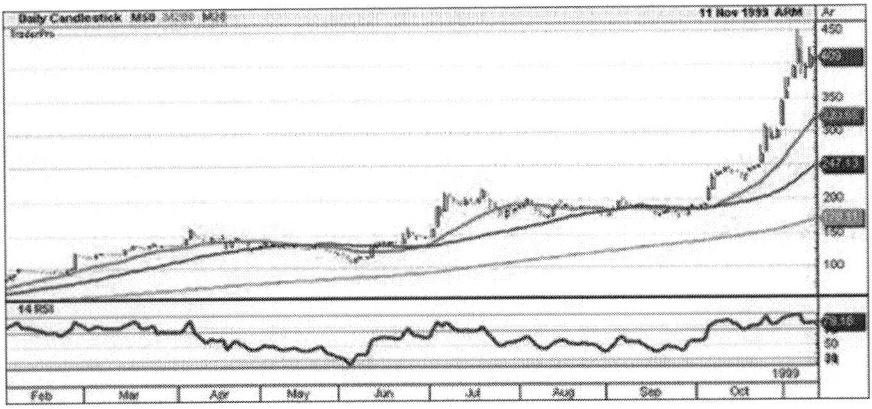

The period from July 1999 to the end of October is particularly interesting, and although I could have gone back a little further back, this is possibly the most helpful part of the chart at this period because it illustrates so many features over such a short space of time. We going into July with an unfilled gap through the last June 80p resistance. It should also be noted that prior to this gap higher we have been treated to support for the shares not only coming in well above the 200 day moving average, but also the 50 day moving average, so much so that there are two support points clear above this feature. There is also a golden cross between the 20 and 50 moving averages going into the start of July.

Outcome

The near instant 20% jump for ARM to start July was less of a surprise than the mini island top above the 100p level on July 19th/July 20th. Of course, normally this may be a sell signal, and there was some downside of a few pence to be had. However, the top of the gap at 102p became the end of day close buy trigger on the basis of the ultra-strong moving average configuration and the way that support for ARM over the summer was coming in 7p and more above previous June resistance. Normal markets will overlap old resistance as new support. Strong markets will find support at old resistance, but it is the really big winners where there is wide open space between the old highs and new lows.

The impasse between the upper 80p's and 100p zone ended with a gap to the upside and an end of day close on October 5th at 107p. This was the big buy signal, with only back below the bottom of the gap at 95p even beginning to delay the upside scenario. Given the way that this was a relatively big percentage stop loss it is just as well that the bulls were never put to the test here.

Payoff

ARM shares doubled within a month. I cannot remember what I was doing in October 1999, but I can be certain that it was not as constructive as being long of this stock.

14. ARM Holdings: During The Bubble

A side effect of going through the charts in this book is that it will inevitably be a Greatest Hits compilation of moments from the past, most of which make the exercise of attaining trading success far more easy than it actually is. While this is not necessarily a bad thing, I would never have got involved if I had not thought it was a perfect pursuit for the lazy. At least some attempt is being made to provide balance. With ARM Holdings in 2000 we have the chart from hell, a period in time that traders/investors of the company would rather forget. Put another way, and with due apology to a musical hero of mine, Ringo Starr, on the otherwise classic album Abbey Road, here we are being serenaded by Octopus's Garden.

The Set Up

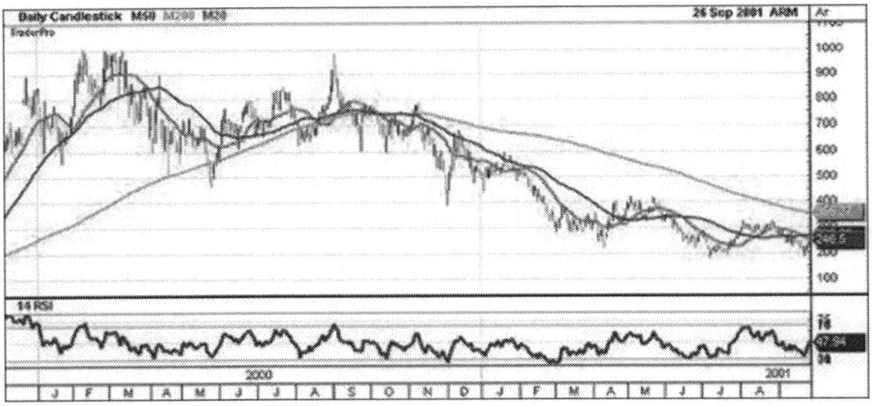

While I am in the mood for metaphors, the financial markets are very much in the Old Testament as opposed to quasi-hippy philosophy of the New Testament in terms of how the financial markets treat those who dare to attempt extracting money from them. It would be pleasant to name check other great faiths of the world in terms of this part of the discourse, unfortunately the risk/reward of any unwitting infringement, especially on the sense of humour front, makes this unattractive. Written guarantees on levels of toleration will be acceptable for any future publication.

As far as ARM in the bubble was concerned, 1999 was a taste of paradise for the bulls with an easy and extended rally from below 100p. This morphed into one of the messiest and complex examples of price action for a stock one might ever have the misfortune of seeing. Perhaps the best way of looking at this is to be aware that even at the best of times the market only gives money with great reluctance. After heaven not only came hell, but the kind of price action designed to ensure that anyone who had enjoyed an easy ride in the shares whether by luck or design from say 100p to 500p, could have given back the gains and more in subsequent attempts to bottom fish/buy on dips. This is the kind of suffering that lasts rather more than forty days and forty nights. The only redeeming feature as far as this part of ARM's charting history is the way that through all the squiggles we have a 50/200 day moving average dead cross no lower than 365p. In no more than five sessions the shares had dipped under 300p.

This, as might have been expected from the dead cross tag, proved to be the beginning of the end of the bull phase in ARM, although not without a last gasp bull trap above 380p and the 200 day moving average. However, it did not stay there long enough to be convincing as a new buy signal, especially as dead crosses effectively trump all in their wake apart from say, bullish RSI divergence and this was not seen here. By April 2001 the stock hit 110.5p and even as recently as the start of 2001 the stock was trading at 77.5p. A one year rally from under 50p to over 500p in 1999-2000 delivered nearly ten years of hard labour for the bulls – a punishment of Biblical proportions.

Payoff

Be it the 1987 Crash, the fall of the Nikkei, the Dot-com Bubble or even ARM's end of millennium rally, it is not always easy to quantify when things have gone over the top and a painful reckoning will follow. Perhaps what is most outstanding regarding the rise and fall of ARM is not only the way it went on for years, but this downward pressure lasted well beyond what the fundamentals might have dictated – there are few who would suggest that the valuation of the chip designer in early 2009 should have been on a par with that of early 1999, but somehow it was.

15. ARM: Ten Years After

It may be strange to some that even though it was widely acknowledged at the time of the Dot-com Bubble that many of the fundamental happenings being bet on were between five and ten years away such as the developed offerings of Amazon (AMZN), Ebay (EBAY) and all the other retailers, mobile technology and assorted internet services we have now, this did not prevent share prices ten bagging within months in many cases.

On the other side of the equation, by the end of the 2000s though it was starting to become evident that traders/investors had not factored in how many advances were being made in the tech area.

The Set Up

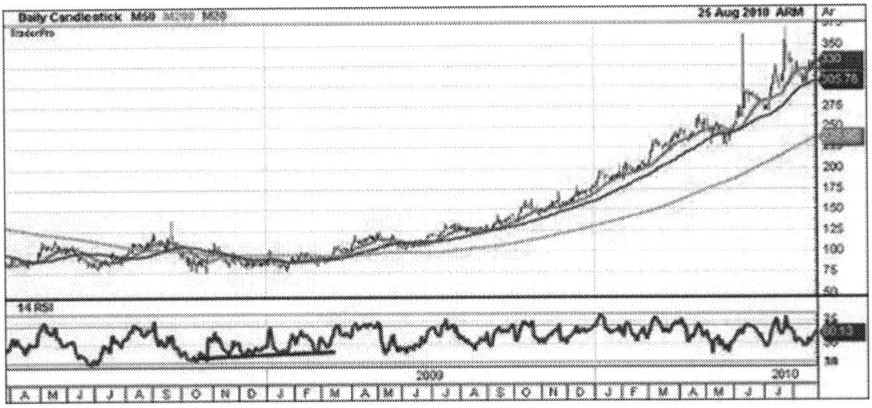

The end of ARM's extended 2000's period in the charting doghouse was not a quick or easy process. The transition had to be made from a super tanker of a bear run to the glory days of years before. Coincidentally, the start of the retest of 2000 resistance started at a very similar share price zone – 80p to 100p, than had been seen in 1999. A point to note on the daily chart is the way that although the bear market here was ended by a golden cross between the 50/200 day moving averages at the end of March 2009 no higher than 105p, it was preceded the previous November by a dead cross. The appearance of this bear signal reminds us that dead crosses can just as often be the end of a sell phase reflecting extremely negative price action and sentiment, as well as the start of a large decline.

Outcome

The most noticeable difference between the late 2000's rally for ARM and the late 1990's affair is that it was not a get rich quick affair with near vertical price action. This was a slow burn to start followed by an acceleration in the pace. Indeed, it was over a year and a half before the type of mega gap to the upside you might have expected given the mania regarding smartphones/iPhones and iPads in 2010. Indeed, the chart of ARM currently is reminiscent of the kind of formation you would expect to see in its US tech sector counterparts such as Apple (AAPL), Research In Motion (RIMM) and Intel (INTC).

Payoff

It may be somewhat cruel to suggest that everything comes to those who wait, particularly as at the time of writing ARM has not yet reached the dizzy heights of 2000. Nevertheless, it may not take great predictive ability whether technical or fundamental to suggest that this will be seen sometime during 2011. If not future updates of this publication may contain a description of one of the best double tops in history.

16. FTSE 100 Death Cross December 2007

A great rule is that the more uncertain the fundamentals are, the more useful/accurate the technicals tend to be. This is obviously helpful in times of crisis and also means that if you are an expert on fundamentals and technicals you are going to be on top of the market at all times. By the end of 2007 the UK was already nearly six months into the credit crunch, but the stock market was still in denial. The charting configuration of the FTSE 100 however delivered one of the simplest and best sell signals ever.

The Set Up

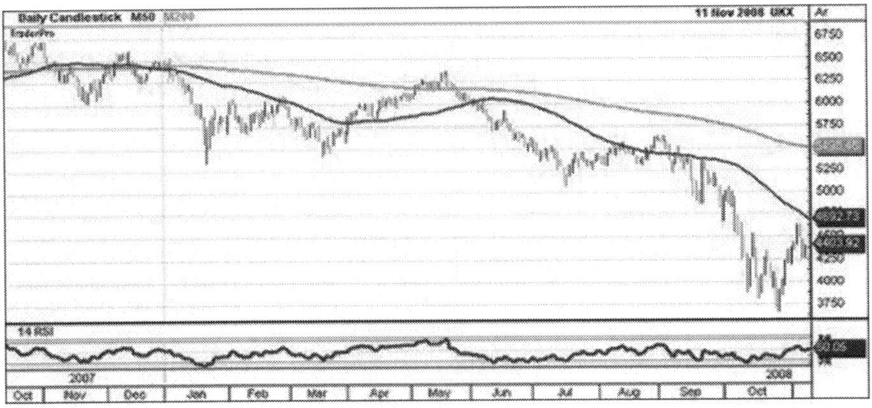

What technical analysts are looking for as far as a death cross is concerned consists of the 50 day and 200 day moving averages – the most influential time periods, crossing over as they are both falling. The only problem, but a very big one, is that usually by the time they have crossed you are 10% or more off the level you would have liked to have sold. But in early 2008 those staring at the cross of death on the open of December 21st who were not still groggy in the wake of the office Christmas parties were faced with an opening UK index level of 6,389. An added wake up call to go short was the unfilled gap up accompanying the sell cross which was eventually filled on the end of day close below it on January. As a final encouragement to dump stocks there was a January 9th gap down – completing a late December/early January island top which turned out to be one of the most correct formations in recent stock market history.

Outcome

The FTSE 100 fell over 1,000 points during January (a decent reminder to always take New Year stock buy tips in the financial media with a pinch of salt). As far as the dead cross signals (plus gap down) this was the perfect example both in terms of a lack of any funny business/delay. In fact, the funny business did not come until May with a final bull trap/exhaustion gap above the then level of the 200 day moving average at 6,170. The UK stock market nearly halved from that point – one that originated with the bear cross between the main moving averages at the start of 2008.

Payoff

If only all charting was this easy. As well as the moving averages we were treated to an island top sell formation which did its job in days. We have a clear message to watch out for the interaction between the main moving averages and chart gaps in all financial markets. We also have an illustration of how amid all the fundamental noise and price action chaos, simple technical analysis signals can clear the correct path for traders.

17. S&P Death Cross/Hindenberg Omen H2 2010

20 years ago when I discovered charting it had all the credibility in the City of London of tarot card or tea leaf reading. In many circles this is still the case, although the advent of broadband internet in the early 2000s as well as browser based trading platforms has meant that now most CFD/spreadbetting firms offer charting packages as a key part of their service. This is especially so given the way that for day traders/swing traders it is very often the case that technical analysis is the main money making weapon. Nevertheless, technical analysis and those who belong to this "profession" still take a backseat to the "serious" fundamental analyst/academics/bankers. Very often in the list of those making predictions for where the market may be in a year's time the charting view is absent. It does not help that of those who are able to offer an opinion, most are either always bullish, always bearish, or simply do not say anything in case they get it wrong and lose their job.

The Set Up

It is perhaps somewhat ironic that the two occasions in the past ten years when I was most correct about the general direction of the stock market were when relatively little reference to underlying charts was made. This is largely because it was so obvious as to be almost unnecessary. The first was in the wake of the 9/11 attacks – a near term bull call, and then at the end of August 2010, also on the buy side. The reason for the latter was that during the silly summer season for the financial markets technical analysis suddenly became the headline news. My immediate suspicion was that this was a last ditch attempt by the smart money in the market to get the not so smart/retail investor out of their long positions, or better still short. Thus far all the Euro bailout domino effect frightening tactics and the general sovereign debt/recessionary bust stories/black swan/Nouriel "$5.5m Manhattan Condo owner" Roubini doomsday scenarios had failed to work.

Therefore the notion was if all else fails, hit the punters with some TA gobbledegook. The first example was the July 2nd dead cross for the S&P and the second the brilliantly named Hindenberg Omen. Unfortunately, for fans of Hindenberg I am not going to even glorify this so called signal by anything more than to say it is a technical set up based on the ratio between new 52 week highs and lows on the NYSE which predicts an imminent crash. To be fair, it probably indicates indecision in a market, the kind of instability that can lead to either a set up for a downturn, a flush out before a rally, or of course nothing much at all. So, it is not that useful, unless you use it as an each way breakout opportunity.

The Outcome

August 15th 2010 was the day of the Hindenberg Omen, and one of my all-time "favourite" strategists Albert Edwards of SocGen (the company that brought us the €4.9bn Jerome Kerviel loss). Mr Edwards predicted a "savage equity downturn," something which went along with a general death of equities vibe over the month. While I may have missed out on correct sell calls in the past, not being able to remember any such nightmare call being correct there appeared to be no chance of this being correct either.

Nevertheless, for a chartist such psychological deduction is secondary to the price action. The possibility of the experts being wrong as far as equities in general and the S&P in the run up to Hindenberg came from a multiple set of factors. First the 50/200 day moving average dead cross sold at the bottom of the range towards 1,000, was followed by a sharp bear trap, bullish RSI divergence rebound and by July 9th the US index had closed above the top of a July 29th gap down at 1,071. At the very least, the position in terms of a possible breakdown for the market appeared difficult unless a bolt from the blue bust such as an EU bailout/banking failure came on tap.

In fact, the dead cross failure – normally a reliable sell signal – was in itself unusual enough to have traders on guard for a rally. This is something which should always be noted, that on most occasions, a failed technical/charting signal can be as strong or even stronger than a successful one. In this instance, the other cross check signals such as RSI/gaps and the like merely keep us on guard for dodgy fundamental calls or simply sentiment getting too bearish relative to these fundamentals. In the summer of 2010, amid predictions of a dire September, this is where we were.

Payoff

The payoff for the S&P and the Dow is that these markets had a glorious September, with the latter delivering its best performance since the world was at the dawn of disaster in 1939. It is to be hoped that the next six years are to be better than the six years following that rally. As well as this the Hindenberg episode underlined the way that while listening to the financial media can throw us off line, it can be very useful to bounce ideas off, especially as far as sentiment is concerned. I would like to thank Mr Edwards for ensuring that my calls were on the right side of the stock market until the end of 2010 and gave me the confidence to judge the late November dip in the wake of the Ireland bailout as a buy opportunity. The golden cross of October 22nd between the 50/200 day moving average had essentially already confirmed the power of the autumn rebound.

On December 14th 2010 it was announced that another Hindenberg Omen had been delivered. Presumably one day the signal will work.

MAJOR MARKETS: MONTHLY CHARTS

18. FTSE 100: 1985-2015?

There have been some steps to ensure that *101 Charts* has a long shelf life, such as delivering analysis on key charting events in recent history and explaining the set ups and preferred strategy at the time in question. But the prediction game is one of nothing ventured, nothing gained. For instance, a bull call in 2000 that the FTSE 100 would hit 10,000 by 2010 while it remained above 6,000 was not a reckless one, particularly as the stop loss of 6,000 was sensible, even though in the end the view was wrong. Indeed, with the 10,000 call one could have added the condition that if 6,000 was broken on a monthly close the target was 3,000. In this way one would have been fully equipped with most of what the past decade delivered.

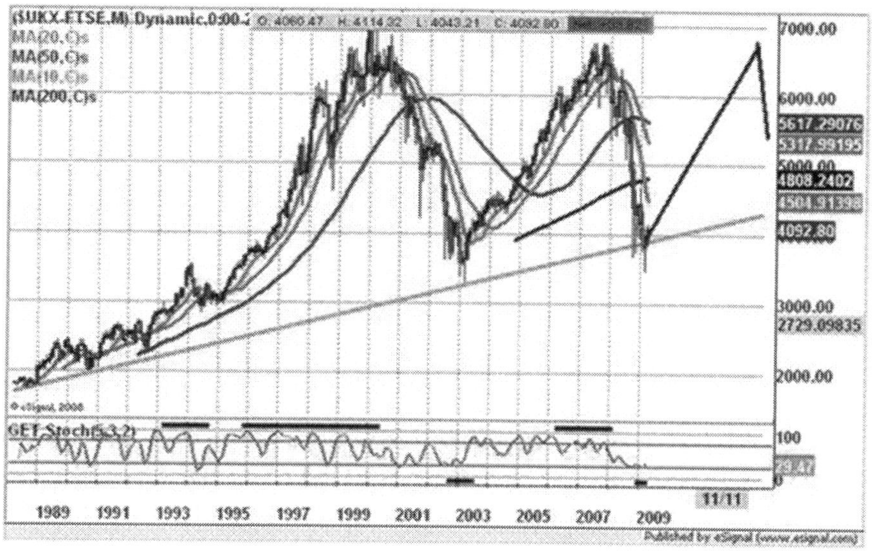

There is a second aspect to attempting to predict the future that it is very often the case that a wrong/failed prediction or set up such as the Hindenberg Omen of August 2010 can be just the type of contrarian signal, like the SocGen equities "bloodbath" call, that may give a cynic the cue to go long of the Dow at the start of September and be on the back of the biggest rally in that month for 71 years. The markets are a curious mix of poker, bridge and chess.

The chart of the FTSE 100 chart shown above appeared in the 2009 Master Investor, and perhaps rather eerily I "knew" that the projection was on the money in terms of the likelihood of a rebound off a 20 year uptrend line running just below 4,000. Unfortunately, this apparent degree of certainty does not happen very often, and far less for all of us than having the feeling we are correct and this not proving to be the case.

The idea behind the projection was that with 2003 and 2009 support at and above previous 1993 resistance means that the FTSE 100 was and is in overall bull mode and is heading higher. After all, old resistance as new support is one of the most reliable technical buy signals.

The second part of the projection was that after two setbacks from just below 7,000 the third visit would see a setback from a peak in this area during 2012. The idea is that the tendency is for at least three tests is that prior to any major breakout – in this case the all-time high the market would "like" to get as many traders sucked in short and this would be done via a partial retreat from the big level. Once a significant number of shorts have been gathered the big breakout can take place. While the FTSE 100 may not come back as low as 5,000 in such a "fakeout" retreat – the early 2011 level of the 1988 uptrend line, somewhere in the upper 5,000 zone is perfectly possible before a big 2013-2015 move high of a similar or even greater magnitude to that of the 1990's bull market.

Of course, there may be myriad events/disasters to chance such a scenario, but while the 1988 support line holds, the constructive pattern is set if only with the 20 year plus uptrend line is its stop loss.

19. Major Markets: S&P 500 From The 1970s Onwards

The chart of the benchmark US stock index is one of the most spectacular in any genre, let alone equities. What makes it most impressive as far as I am concerned is the way that this was a mainstream index that rose in an almost exponential fashion, something you might only expect to see from the resources or technology area. While one would not wish to be partisan (not too much anyway) fans of Reaganomics can certainly take a bow here. Even with the Crash of 1987 this was still an awe inspiring performance, and it is easy to see how the idea that stocks were as safe as houses (bad analogy) and represented an asset class everyone should be a part of, grew from this era. Ironically, given the static stock market conditions from 2000-2010 when interest rates and inflation were low, it would appear that both interest rates and inflation nearer to 10% than 5% is better for stocks, at which time equity indices becomes something of a hedge against inflation – tending to rise ahead of prices.

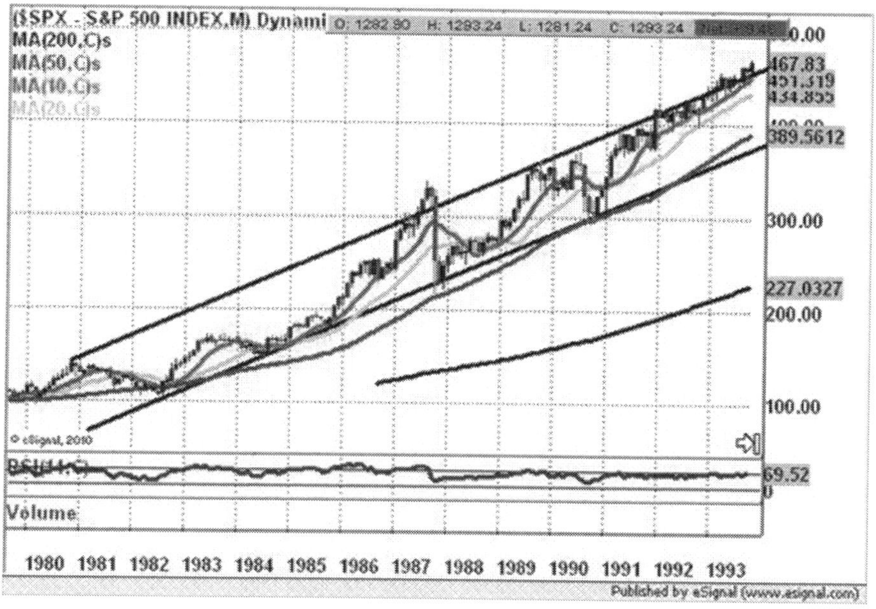

The charting points to note on the monthly chart of the S&P apart from the massive gains are the way that the 1987 Crash was the correction of an overshoot of the top of a rising 1981 price channel on the monthly chart. The rebound was a relatively straightforward affair from the floor of the channel near 230. The surprise is the way that the 1990 setback for US stocks was a painful affair, but one that did not make the history books.

There was also the message to buy and hold investors that you could ignore crashes and other periods of stock market weakness as they would "always" bounce back. This was the case in both 1987 and 1990. By the early 1990s it may have looked to some that the S&P had hit the top of the range as far as the 1981 channel. But if the Reagan years brought riches, with Clinton things went into outer space up to the end of the decade. As is usually the case with the markets, there had to be a payback.

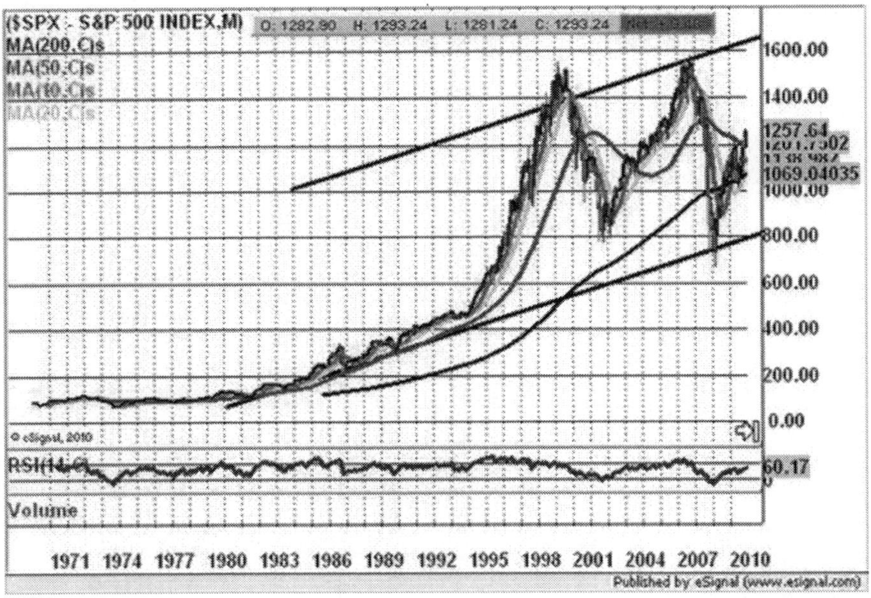

This came in the form of two 50% retracements from the highs for the S&P, with a double bear trap from 2008/9. On this basis alone one would be keen on calling up this market to 1,500 plus all-time highs, not based solely on any great predictive powers, but on the general rule that a bear trap usually leads back to the last major resistance. Such joy should lie in story for 2011/12, but the big question would be what happens after that? Once again the likelihood is that after a decade of bucking bronco price action – designed to scare out the buy and hold brigade, the upside – probably 50% upside, is favoured especially after the painful bear trap effect of the immediate post Credit Crunch period.

20. Crude (WTI) Monthly: From The 1980s

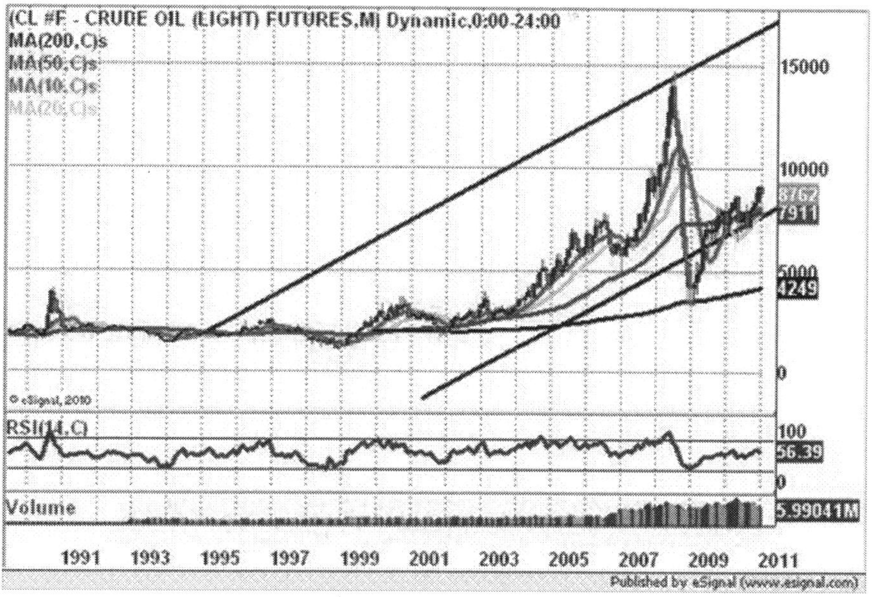

Something strange about Crude Oil as a market is that over recent decades we have seen it blow hot and cold in terms of the headline making influence it has. It has effectively alternated between being of life and death importance to a market which has for extended periods been something of a sleeping giant even in terms of volatility and newsflow.

Of course, the cliché as far as commodities in general and WTI in particular is the way that they are supposed to be so unpredictable. What can be seen from the 30 year charting view is the way that there have essentially been two main periods for this market, a $10-$40 range until 2003, and then a $40-$140 plus range since. The standout was not so much the spike to $147 in 2008, but the way that this market came back to test the former $40 resistance as new support. If there was ever an advertisement for the power of technicals this was it. Just in case you missed the idea that old resistance would become new support there was also the 200 month moving average now at $42 – a feature which many years from now could feature as support again.

But until then the trajectory for this market may be mapped via a rising trend channel which is based at the 50 week moving average in place at $79 and in place since 1994. That this line holds is critical to the idea that we are due at least a partial and significant retest of the 2008 resistance. Charting rules dictate there should be another look at this spike over the next few years, especially if 2010 resistance quickly becomes new support in 2011. The nightmare scenario for the bulls is that the $80 zone is lost and there is a return to the 200 month line. This seems very unlikely, but with WTI being open minded is an obligation.

21. Gold Monthly Chart: The "Brown Bottom" And Beyond

While the daily chart perspective can provide a detailed insight into how key turning points were negotiated in a stock or market, one of the best aspects of the longer timeframe is to provide an insight into what the long term trend is/has been, as well as allowing the chartist to project forwards, if only by means of a trend channel.

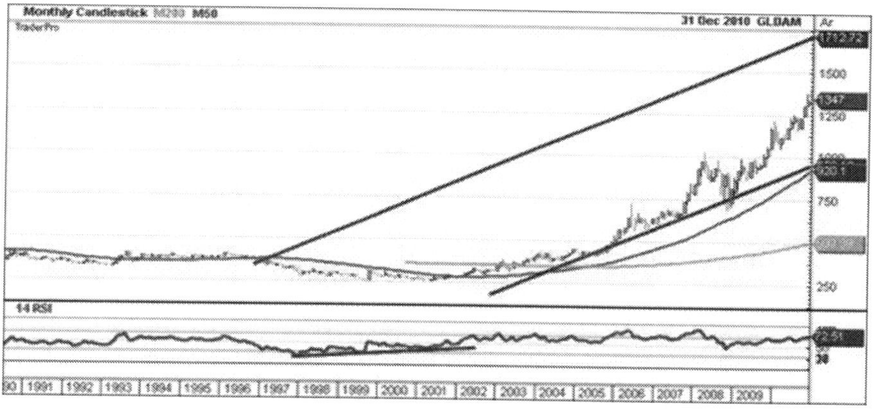

As well as the 1997 trend channel drawn on the month chart of Gold, what has been very helpful on the extended timescale is the 50 month moving average and using it in a very simple way. This was broken in January 2002 at $281 – just after former UK Chancellor Gordon Brown completed his sale of the bulk of the UK's Gold reserves, and the rest is history if you are a bull. Indeed, it may be sensible to look at this market with the same indicator as a dynamic stop loss. While it could very well be the case that in say, 2015 Gold is up at $3,000 and the consensus is that it could go to $5,000, a monthly close back below the 50 month moving average really has to be regarded at that point as a sell signal. As of the end of 2010 it stood some $400 below the Gold price, so on the face of it there was little chance of the moving average being breached in a year or two or even more. In fact, the top of the 1997 price channel shown here suggests that by the end of 2012 the metal could hit $2,000 an ounce, while a $1,100 support line hold . (See also Commodities Corner).

STOCK WATCH: THE FALL OF THE GIANTS

22. RBS Gets Shredded

The Set Up

What a relief all round it is that the FSA found no wrong doing at RBS in the run-up to the spectacular collapse, following the ill-fated idea to take over ABN Amro. In fact, this particular failure has been put down not to any criminal wrong doing but to bad decision making. If only the law took such a 21st century attitude towards muggers, sex offenders, murderers and George Michael's inability to take a taxi. Presumably the Wikileak that will emerge on the investigation into the fall of RBS is that a court trial at this point really would have brought the bank down.

Of course, among the millions of words written about RBS over the past couple of years, there has perhaps not been too much fixating on how well the management of the Dutch bank did in cashing in just before the credit crunch struck. While decimated shareholders at the UK bank may beg to disagree, I have taken the view that the disaster of ABN Amro was simply an attempt to repeat the highly successful NatWest takeover in 2000. It could be said that the chance of the ABN deal failing was once in a generation, and on this occasion the Fates did their worst.

Outcome

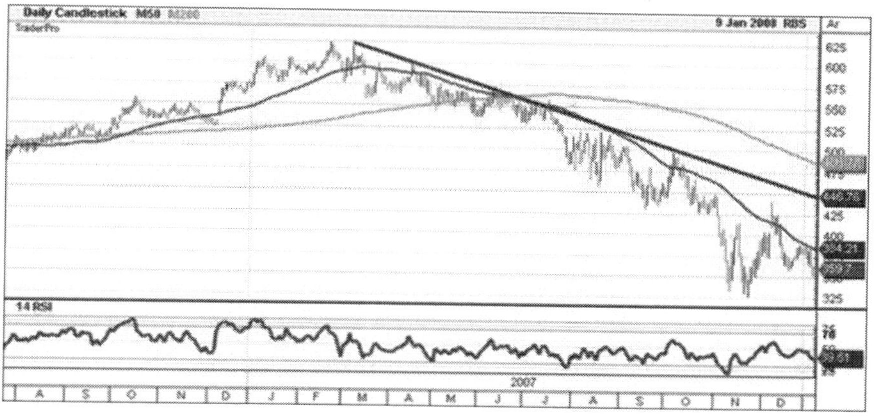

In honour of the deal too far from Sir Fred Goodwin's former bank we have two charts, essentially a before and after to investigate. The first is the typical failure to rebound off the trend governing 200 day moving average, and then the way that after the breakdown in August new resistance came in well below former support at 520p and above from late 2006. Also to be noted is the way that a line of resistance was well in place from February by the time the 200 day line was lost in the summer.

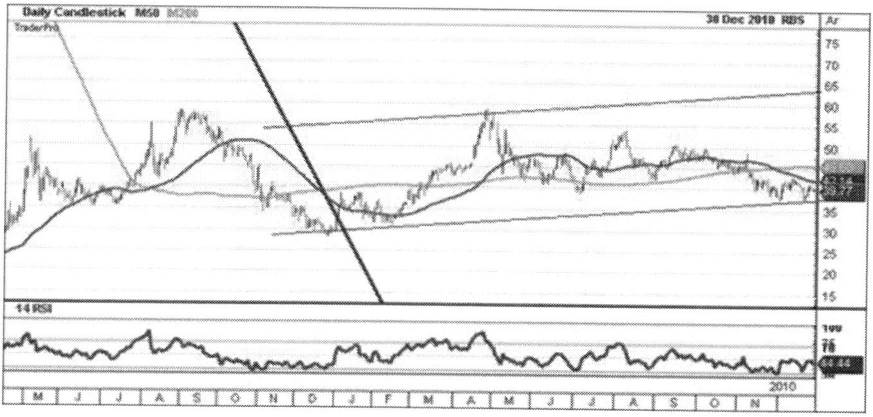

Stepping forward to 2010, which ended with the "acquittal" of the former management of RBS, we see the share price less than 10% of where we left it three years before. But what can also be seen is the way that the early 2007 resistance line projection broke the price action in Q1 2010. Perhaps this will provide a long awaited trend change toward lasting recovery? The best that can be said in the meantime is that since Q1 2009 the shares have been crawling up a rising trend channel currently based just below 40p. There is the opportunity for brave bottom fishers to call the low. Purely on a support/resistance basis resistance 60p needs to be cleared on a weekly or preferably monthly close before the crisis for this bank can finally be deemed over.

Payoff

Given the way that it may be everyone except the aforementioned management of RBS knew at the time that the ABN deal was a mistake, it could very well be argued that the recent history of this bank represented one of the best shorting opportunities in history. Unless or until the three year resistance line is broken we still have a sell on strength on our hands, with the bank's exposure to Euro bailout victims/contenders keeping the bulls at bay, just as effectively as the Christmas bankers' bonus season undermines the PR of the group with respect to its 83% shareholder – the taxpayer.

For a while in 2010 it appeared that the UK's Prudential (PRU) would repeat the same mistake with its David and Goliath bid for AIA. But fortunately the insurer swallowed its pride and backed off, rather than risk self-destruction. Ironically, given the lessons learnt from RBS, and a rising stock market, the Pru may actually have got away with it.

23. Lloyds Banking: Getting Hitched With HBOS

The Set Up

If it had been my decision there would have been no bailouts of banks or anyone else during the 2008-2009 period, even if the final outcome is that the taxpayer turns a profit. Saving banks is simply not the role of Government.

Even Lehman Brothers went down and the world did not end, proving that the idea of "too big to fail" is reckless, unfair, and not that many care about the concepts anymore, also anti-democratic and immoral – especially as savers and hard workers have to pay for the wilful greed of risk takers. My explanation of the too big to fail is Governments and especially politicians giving themselves a dragon to slay to win (or lose) votes. Perhaps more importantly it provides an excuse to raise taxes in order to make The State fatter, as well as reveal where and how much cash the general public actually has.

For banks such as RBS, Lloyds and HBOS the solution could have been to simply pay off the deposit holders and start the sector again. True, we would have had less choice as to where to put our savings, or get a mortgage from for a while, but with rates at 0% for savers and banks still not lending I doubt whether many would have noticed the difference. There would have been a lot of former bank employees and bonus grabbers unemployed for a while, but such highly skilled and motivated people can always find a job.

Instead, when HBOS did a Northern Rock Prime Minister Gordon Brown saved the world by arranging a shotgun wedding between Lloyds and HBOS, not only defying all the competition rules but also illustrating how meaningless they are in the first place.

Outcome

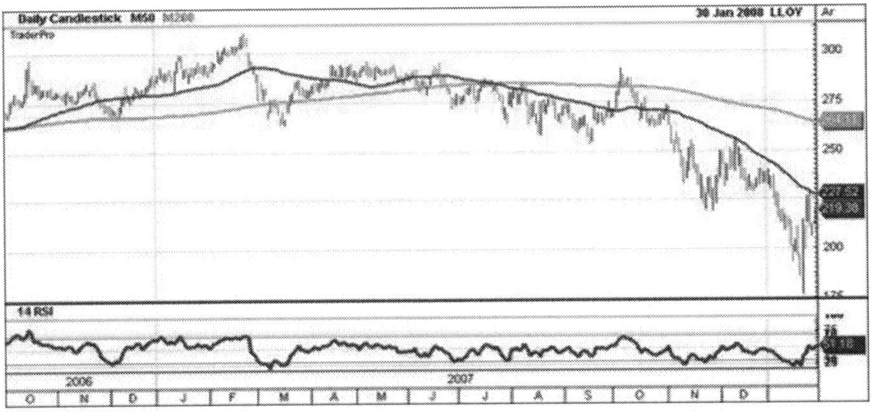

The charting importance of the 200 day moving average cannot be overstated. My estimate is that correct use of just this indicator can be the base for every investor. The assumption of a rising trend from a price cross above a rising 200 day line works its magic in all but the most unusual situations. Lloyds being coerced into merging with HBOS was not enough to break the concept, or even the moving of the goalposts shorting ban of September 2008.

It would be appropriate to call the decline of Lloyds a supertanker affair. This is on the basis that the turnaround from brought to bear trend happened over a period of months, and was delivered via a series of charting/technical "goodbyes." The first was a February 2007 gap to the downside, with the top of the gap at £2.86. For traders at the time only an end of day close back above the top of this gap negated the idea that the shares were a sell into strength. Over three years later this gap has still not been filled and on this basis alone one could theoretically have been short of the shares ever since.

But there were games to be played with the 200 day moving average, with a brief dip below the line in March and then an extended decline from June onwards. By August the 200 day line was falling – from this point onwards we were really on red alert for a long-term decline in the banking stock. I would suggest that those owning stock screening software such as Updata's TraderPro run regular sweeps of leading stocks to determine which names have shares where the 200 day line have just started to turn up/down.

In fact, the big sell signal was the attempt to clear the 200 day line on a sustained basis in October – following three months of consistent 200 day line declines. Those owning Lloyds shares should really have exited at this point. For the bears it was a clear run from October 2007 to September 19th 2008 – just after Lehman's collapse. The night before the FSA had issued a ban on shorting leading financial shares. Hedge funds moaned, and should have sued the FSA for any losses, but of course no jury would ever award a penny to a hedge fund. Instead, many leading stocks surged by 20% and more thus offering one of the best shorting opportunities in years. The usual rule is to trade against the direction of any intervention – the authorities wanted the markets to go up, so you go short. I would call this the Soros Rule in honour of his shorting of Sterling as the UK tried and failed to stay within the ERM in 1992. Buying the Yen as Japan attempts to weaken its currency, and shorting peripheral Eurozone bonds to force bailouts is clearly the fashionable Soros trade currently.

For Lloyds on September 19th 2008 we were treated to a spike to the 200 day moving average at 182p, with a day high of 184p and hence a great sell signal, just a couple of days after the announcement of a merger with HBOS. This was arguably the biggest week in the recent history of the financial markets coinciding with the fall of Lehman's, the bailout of AIG and the Bank of America/Merrill Lynch merger. Given all the fundamental noise the benefit of just using a chart and a moving average is clear. Shares in Lloyds remained a sell, staying below their 200 day line until July 2009 at 50p. I cannot think of a simpler way of dealing with the markets in that this break above the 50p level was the first major signal the worst may be over.

Payoff

As things stand the Lloyds/HBOS merger has been labelled a success – maintaining the dignity of the UK banking sector. Those who like myself were against the deal would point to the way that with a 5% spread between deposit and mortgage rates, carte blanche in terms of charges and lending policy, even BCCI would have succeeded. To compensate there was a mighty shorting signal and a smooth ride down for those who did not like the Lloyds/HBOS arrangement and now while a two year trendline from the start of 2009 at 60p remains in place we have a tentative bottom fishing opportunity while no further bailouts are required.

STOCK WATCH: BORN IN THE USA

Although I have always been more focused towards U.K. stocks, it has to be admitted that especially in the technology area the likes of Apple (AAPL) and Google (GOOG) are where the fundamental and charting excitement really lies. The financial area is no less exciting with Lehman Brothers having already appeared in *101 Charts* and Citigroup (C) and AIG among those in the frame in the wake of the economic crisis from 2007 onwards. It therefore seems appropriate to check out some of the heroes at key points in their progress.

24. Apple (AAPL): The iPod Bull Run

Shares in Apple at the end of 2010 are now well over $300. In early 2003 – not that long ago – Apple was trading below $10 and a respectable maker of pretty looking PCs which did not crash as much as those using the Windows operating system from Microsoft. But it was the iPod that delivered the fundamental change at the end of 2001 with the effect starting to kick in from the start of the Baghdad Bounce in March 2003.

The Set Up

In the late 1990s you could have picked up Apple shares for around four dollars, with a peak in the wake of the dot-com bubble over $30. Three years later and the shares were back to the $7 zone. As is usually the case that before every major move there is a countermove offered in order to shake off those who correctly anticipated it, and more importantly to ensure no one is in there by accident. In the case of Apple this came via a bear trap below $6.50 in April. In fact, what is incredible here is how many classic technical signals are at play in the wake of the bear trap.

Outcome

The first buy signal here at Apple is that we were treated to bullish divergence in the RSI window between the $6.46 and $6.36 lows in mid-April. Those who were not tempted to bottom fish could have then waited for the black 200 day moving average then under $7.40 to be broken. This was not only broken on May 5th, but there was a gap above the 200 day line. Such gaps are one of the strongest buy signals in the TA armoury, and considering that this turnaround at Apple was a once in a lifetime event, lives up to this tag. As if this was not enough May 15th delivered a golden cross between the 50 and 200 day moving averages, and then one of the most robust of technical buy signals. This was followed by a higher low above both the 50 and 200 day lines, acting as a final confirmation that a sustained move to the upside was likely to follow. Taking this situation forward there was a bounce off the 200 day line in December 2003 just below $10, a continuation signal. There followed two unfilled gaps in 2004, another 200 day bounce in March 2006, with the sell signal finally coming in May 2006 at $63 when the 200 day line was finally lost. All this was not too bad for such simple analysis.

Payoff

I could go on with the Apple story, which is a great one technically, in protest at the lack of flash support for iPhones and iPads which is a disaster for anyone wanting to look at Beatles.com and most (currently) financial trading websites. Nevertheless, the multiple buy signals seen in spring 2003 for Apple were transformational, and have been repeated on many occasions before and since. Single digit penny shares in oil & gas explorers and precious metals groups are where you might expect to see an Apple style turnaround at the moment.

25. Google (GOOG): The Start of Trading

The Set Up

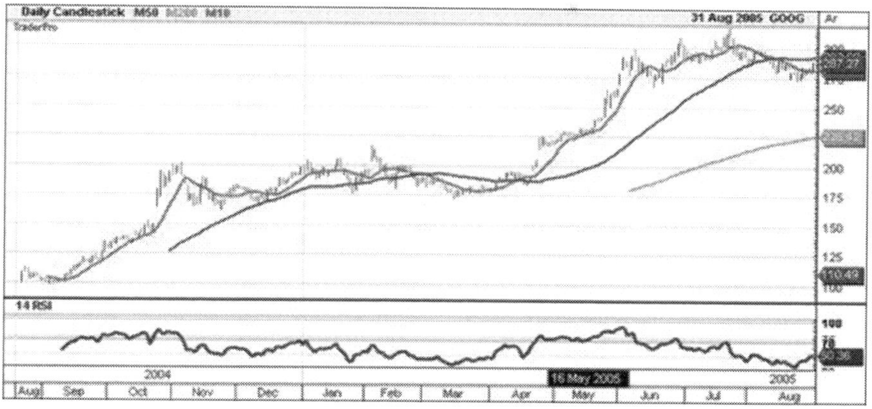

Something which strikes me about both Apple and Google is the way that both companies seem to have come from the near future via a time machine – two/three years ahead, and delivered their technology to an eager public. August 19th 2004 was the day that the internet search engine came to market, and of course it now seems incredible that anyone doubted it would be anything other than a resounding success. But as much as anything else, the event does provide an insight into how to handle an IPO from a charting perspective. There is a certain merit in being able to anticipate a market's moves from the time when there is minimal historic data to go on. Indeed, with banks not lending – they don't like doing so at the bottom of the cycle – it may very well be that sharpening skills as far as trading IPOs is something worth doing.

While there may be the temptation to use an hourly/intraday timeframe in order to trade a stock which is new to the market, and therefore get on board on the day or within a few days of a company listing, the more conservative/safer approach is to wait on an opening day range break. This may sound fraught, but surprisingly what the opening range is and the behaviour after it is broken tend to be reasonably consistent.

Outcome

For Google it can safely be said that most traders would have been looking/hoping for a break to the upside. The opening day range was $96-

$104. The options were to buy on the second day after an end of day close through $104 or wait on a break of the August $113 high by September 16th, by which time we had the rising ten day moving average to act as a trailing stop loss. Only an end of day close back below $96 would have been a sell signal strong enough to abandon the bull argument at Google.

Payoff

Years after its IPO Google remains a classic trading stock across all timeframes, and provides technical fireworks on regular occasions. It helped that such a volatile stock delivered a relatively straightforward open to its life on the market, with the share price doubling within three months. Getting in at the ground floor in this way should be remembered as one of the easier ways of building a portfolio.

26. Citigroup (C): A Successful Bailout

The Set Up

Citigroup is another of the too big to fail/moral hazard brigade that I would have allowed to fail on the basis it was simply unfair to save Citi and not save every other company caught out by the crisis. This is even though the US taxpayer has managed to turn a $12bn profit on the collapse. But what is $12bn these days . . . ? There is a technical reason for the stock's appearance in *101 Charts*, adding to the fundamental news that George Soros and the hedge fund brigade were reported as having piled into Citi in early 2010 via as much as half a billion shares. While this may be enough for most of us to simply pile in as well, there are charting aspects here which apply to the aftermath of big sell offs and enable a technician to determine whether a bottom fish or a relapse could be due.

Outcome

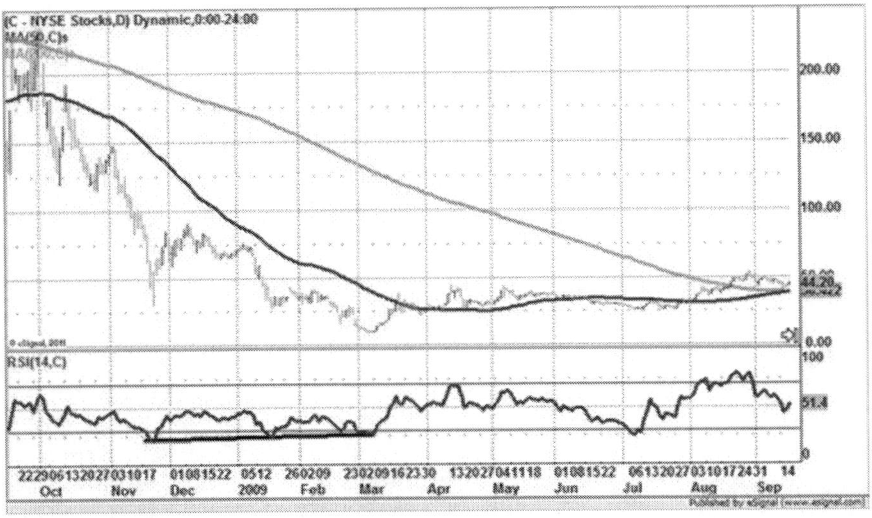

This is daily chart timeframe for Citigroup – and we have an illustration of what is a classic slow burn long opportunity **during 2008-9.** The hedge fund buying here in early 2010 would have coincided with a price no higher than $35 in February. This coincided with bullish divergence in the RSI window between the December and February lows. In fact, you could have beaten the hedge funds by many months buying off the back of bullish divergence between November 2008 support and March 2009 lows at no higher than $20.

But it is actually an uptrend line drawn from November 2008 in the RSI window which governs the recovery here. The longer this oscillator line remains in place, the greater the chance of an acceleration to the upside. Perhaps better than this is the way that the oscillator trend should provide an early warning signal in terms of the two year consolidation breaking down below the 50 week moving average zone of $38. The normal pattern would be that the RSI line would break well ahead of the price of Citigroup shares falling significantly, thereby acting as a sell alert.

Payoff

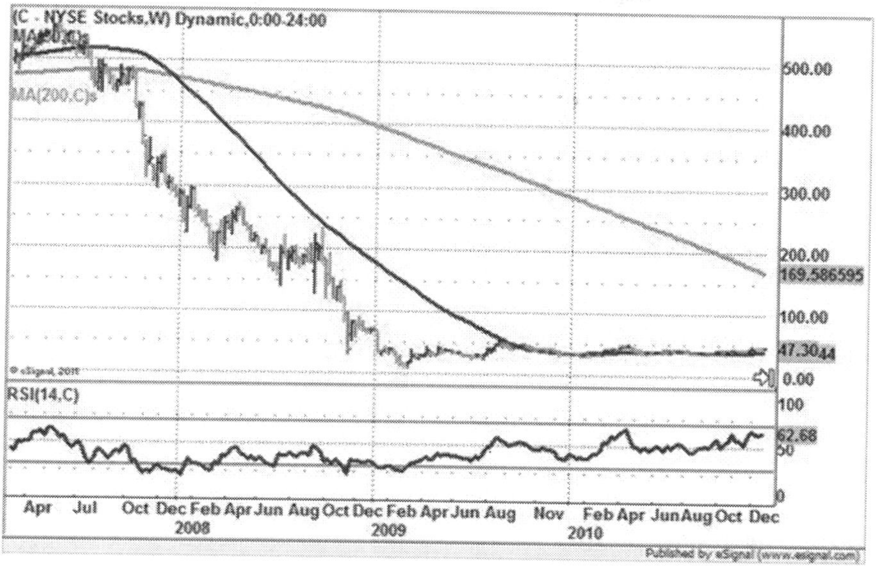

Peace of mind can be useful for those attempting to catch a falling knife in the markets, or even go against the grain of sentiment. As far as Citigroup is concerned, cautious diehards who are not satisfied with a two year recovery or a fistful of hedge fund investors may decide it is worth only going long here when/if August 2009 neckline resistance at $54.30 is broken – an event which could be a couple of years away. I would not blame them.

BOLTS FROM THE BLUE

27. British Airways Ahead Of 9/11

Cynics would argue that ahead of any surprise/shock event that a trader has a 50/50 chance of facing the correct direction. I would not wish to argue with this. But a survey of unexpected events in the recent past can at least provide an insight into what the dangers and benefits are of being involved at such times and in their aftermath.

The Set Up

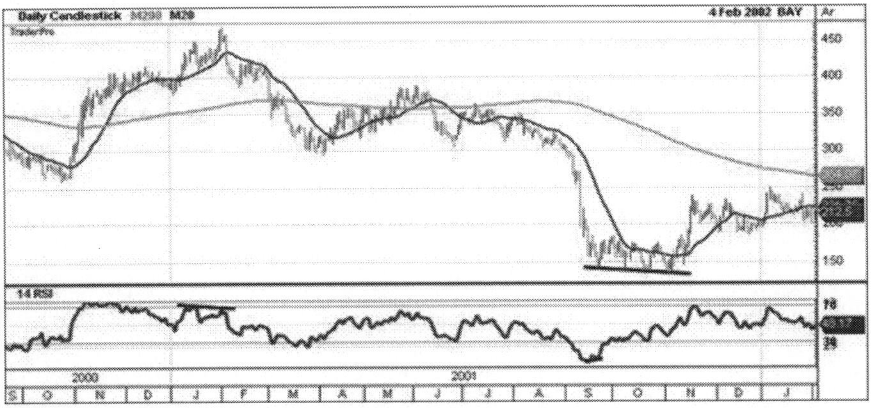

The conspiracy theorists have suggested that the reason that airline stocks were falling ahead of 9/11 was because someone had the inside track on what was about to happen. Of course, the people who orchestrated it did and there may have been the odd leak . . .

But it was also the case that in early autumn 2001 US economic fears were knocking BA shares aggressively, with the explanation as to why the stock was falling like a stone being the forthcoming FTSE 100 reshuffle on September 12th. Tracker funds would have been bailing out of the shares as it became increasingly likely that the company would be evicted from the blue chip index.

Outcome

Before I was reminded that BA was demoted from the FTSE 100 on September 12th 2001 what seemed most suspicious about the price action here was not the halving of the share price in the weeks up to 9/11 but the way that almost immediately after the event there was a bullish divergence buy signal. This now appears to be nothing more sinister than the usual stock market phenomenon of selling the rumour/buying the news profit taking. Nevertheless, one had to have nerves of steel to get involved in airline stocks over this period as for all we knew at the time there could have been more aviation related attacks.

Payoff

Like the run up to 9/11 for the indices it would have been difficult for traders to have been anything other than short, with the eerie coincidence of the demotion of BA from the FTSE 100 due the following day. Therefore it is difficult to suggest in this instance anything other than that the technicals forecast future events, as the shares were in deep sell mode for multiple reasons already.

28. BP: The Curse Of Macondo

Although the case for the prosecution would have us believe that the fatal Deepwater Horizon rig explosion and leak was part of chronic safety issues at BP, in the end it may be that the lasting damage to the oil giant came from the public relations disaster which was of the Fawlty Towers variety. In the UK this may have been tolerable, but in the US with the Obama administration aiming to show its mettle for once, BP was hung out to dry. At least the incumbent CEO Tony Hayward was able to act as the fall guy and sail off into the sunset (literally). Having a new American CEO should ensure that any further fallout is dissipated without incident.

The Set Up

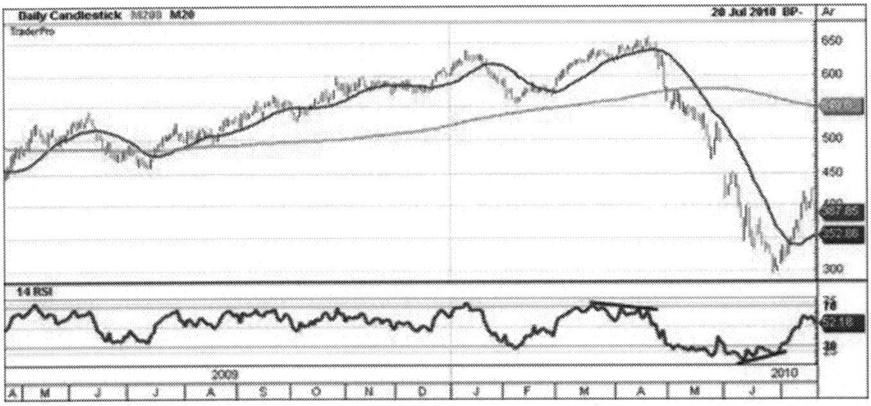

Presumably it was a coincidence that on the day of the disaster April 20th, BP shares were just about to test two year highs at 657p. Indeed, the initial assurance from BP that we were looking at a contained event meant that the following day BP hit a new four year intraday high of 658p. But it was downhill from there as it became clear that Deepwater was to be a long, drawn out affair. Technically there was also more on offer than a narrow bull trap double top. Presumably, no one knew that there was going to be a well disaster for BP at the end of April. However, the higher April price highs versus March delivered bearish divergence in the RSI window – the price action had already delivered a sell signal.

Payoff

We have to assume that the clear bearish divergence for BP ahead of the April 2010 explosion was a coincidence, but it was not only a coincidence but something of a technical gift, with the shares halving in less than two months. Those who did not get on board in the immediate aftermath of the incident had the May 5th and May 6th intraday high failures below the 200 day moving average then at 580p as an additional call to go short. In fact, given the way that BP is such a core part of portfolios this is one situation where charting delivers personal wealth preservation rather than merely being a way of speculating for "greedy" purposes. After all, the dividend was cut soon after.

29. BP: Out Of Deepwater

The Set Up

The great BP share price fall of 2010 was started by a fundamental disaster and bearish RSI divergence, and was also ended by the RSI coming as bullish divergence. For those looking at the stock at the time we had the feeling that the lows were imminent from the start of June after the gap down, but the bear run just would not end.

Outcome

There was a temporary jump from 350p to 379p – perfectly tradeable off the back of the first bullish divergence of the month in weeks 1 and 2, but the big buy was delivered after the June 29th low which was followed by a gap higher the day after. This provided a long entry in the 320p-330p region to start July with the choice of money management being the bottom of the gap at 307p on an end of day close basis or simply an end of day close back below the ten day moving average. On this occasion it was enough to deliver over 80p of profit for those with the nerves to stay in place.

Payoff

The criticism of many methods of technical analysis is that signals are lagging/late. Divergence is strong and quick enough to provide entry signals close to market end points, with the lagging indicators such as moving averages there to provide dynamic support levels and/or trailing stop loss levels.

30. De La Rue: A License To Print Funny Money

The Set Up

For many of us the idea that a company literally has a licence to print money should put it in their unassailable position fundamentally. Unfortunately some staff at banknote printer De La Rue decided to put this theory to the test by allegedly forging the specifications of the paper being used. The result of this in the autumn of 2010 was a rather inevitable plunge in the share price, the revelation of a £35 million charge and uncertainty over the future of the group given the clear damage to its reputation. In fact, the year ended with a couple of the takeover offers on the table leaving technicians with a classic story of a surprise decline followed by an equally swift recovery. This episode is a useful case study in how to approach companies which are a volatile mix of fundamental news flow and price action.

Outcome

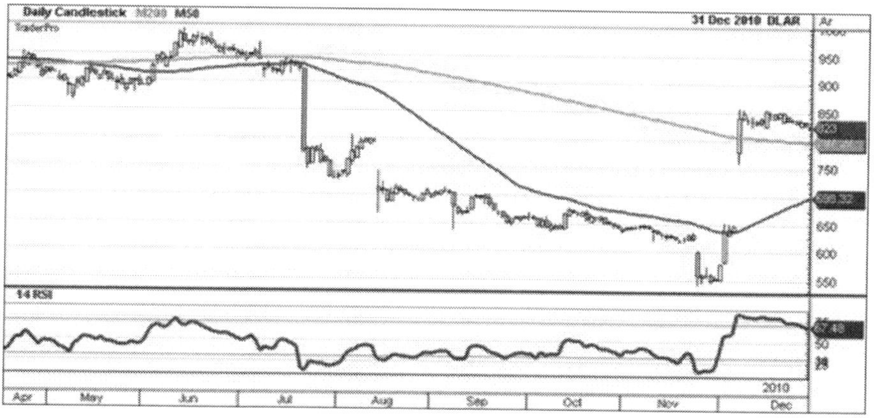

The announcement of the bombshell from De La Rue on July 20th had actually been foretold by a somewhat mysterious chart gap down below the 50 day moving average, meaning that those following a standard technical practise of selling the gap up to £9.39 could actually have fluked being in the correct direction ahead of the official warning. Ironically, the next clear signal for the stock was a bullish divergence signal presenting itself in the last few days of August below £7.50. Here there was up to 50p upside towards the 50 day moving average which had capped the price before a warning a month earlier.

While uncertainty remained on the fundamental basis, it was interesting that if there were signals they were generally on the buy side, such as another bullish divergence play in early October. But perhaps the best signal of war here came on December 1st with the gap to the upside completing an island bottom, something which snapped a RSI line of resistance at oversold 30. If this all sounds somewhat obscure, it was not obscure enough for me to spot the shares as a buy at 574p for Zaks-TA.com members.

Payoff

Of course the two bid approaches that followed the island bottom/RSI trendline break were most welcome, but not entirely a surprise given that the only end game on the fundamental basis for the banknote group is to lose its independence, and a technical basis the island formation so rare and so strong that significant events tend to follow.

31. African Barrick Gold: As Thick As Thieves

The Set Up

Tanzania focused miner African Barrick Gold's website contains the following:

> "Our staff is our single most important asset. Employees are respected, valued and supported in the workplace. As part of our commitment to our staff, we are committed to delivering the following:

Generous compensation for our employees. In Tanzania, African Barrick Gold employees earn, on average, three times the minimum wage

- A safe, gender equal and non-discriminatory working environment
- Empowering all employees through the company's Courageous Leadership training programme
- Encouraging personal responsibility and accountability and provides meaningful performance feedback."

Outcome

On October 14th African Barrick Gold announced it had suspended 40% of the mining department at its Buzwagi mine in Tanzania following a fuel theft. Clearly, there are times when even paying staff three times the minimum wage just is not enough.

The charting set up on the downside was a gap below the 50 day moving average then at 590p. While it could be argued that the price action was flailing before the announcement as if readying itself for bad news, there was nothing untoward within the pattern one might expect for a mining stock. The gap through the moving average delivered an extended period of weakness that one might have expected – as seen above at De La Rue. Strangely, the end of the bear move came in the form of a gap to the upside, just above the 50 day moving average at 560p to start December, echoing what we saw at the banknote printer – but without the aid of any bid approaches. A bear trap leading to a break of the last major resistance – 600p plus is the usual outcome one would expect here.

Payoff

In both African Barrick and De La Rue we have good examples of what to expect when the unexpected happens. The gap down after the shock announcement (a sign of traders being wrong footed), price action below the bottom of the gap. Bullish divergence ideally then comes in followed by a gap up to officially end the bear period.

32. Connaught Gets Caught Out

Connaught (CNT) was a perfectly respectable FTSE 250 support services group to the social housing sector, one that was booming during the final phase of New Labour/Gordon Brown's administration. It enjoyed the perfect mix of the bloated sacred cow of the Welfare State as well as the aftermath of the 2008 financial crisis pushing more of the UK population away from the private housing sector.

The social housing part of the group took the full impact of first the Labour Government warning on the need for expenditure cuts in this area, and the rather theatrical way that the Coalition threatened to make even more swingeing cuts. The irony now at the end of 2010 is that Connaught is no longer with us. But apart from rearranging a few spending deckchairs on the Titanic deficit and causing students to be even more revolting than ever, the public sector is apparently spending even more than ever. Blaming the previous Government, bankers and the crumbling EU has so far been the main weapon against the deficit and so Connaught may have died in vain.

The Set Up

A gap down through the 200 day moving average is usually a serious sell signal. If this does not signal the start of an extended bear phase it can at least be the start of a volatile period either side of the 200 day line. But the killer for the bulls is almost always a test of the 200 day moving average as resistance shortly after – typically three to six months after the gap down. This has been seen in some of the big casualties of the recent past with Lehman Brothers (LEHMQ), RBS Lloyds doing this very deliberately on their daily charts. In fact, this is normally in the aftermath of a gap down through the 200 day moving average – in RBS's case it was a gap down through the 50 day moving average that was the kiss of death.

For Connaught the initial part of the one-two sell signal came in December 2009. I have subsequently read rather strange reports that irregular but legal accounting methods were undermining the company going into H1 2010, but that a bullish April update (how ahead of the uncertainty May General Election?) lead to the completion of a 250p to 340p rally.

For all we knew this would be the end of Connaught's woes, and it is unfortunately the kind of false dawn remission which can be deadly for bottom fishers without sound money management. There were three clues that this might not be the case – the bearish RSI divergence between the May/June highs, a triple top in May/June above 330p and the failure for the price action below the 200 day moving average. Unfortunately, unless you had already decided that Connaught was doomed in the wake of the June 22nd Emergency Budget the one third fall in the stock on June 25th might have caught you off guard. From then until the end when the company was forced to call in the administrators the 20 day moving average was the best that the stock price could reach.

Payoff

In some ways Connaught was too obviously a sell, and such a volatile mover that the degree of difficulty here made it a good bear situation to learn from but not necessarily a great one to trade at the time. The 250p-340p spring rally was particularly painful to the short argument and indeed left the impression until even a relatively late stage that Connaught was a stock to bottom fish

CHARTING GIFTS: AT A GLANCE WINNERS/LOSERS

33. Yell (YELL): A Cry For Help April 2007

I suppose the wrong questions to ask as far as directories group Yell is concerned are how it managed to amass £4bn in debt at worst just from producing the Yellow Pages, and even more importantly, how it manages to keep going?

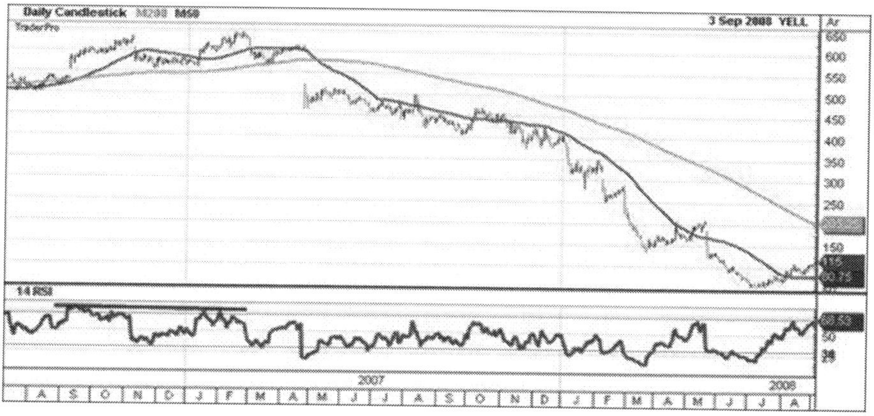

From a technical perspective the big turning point on the daily chart of the stock came in early 2007, what we now know was the beginning of the end of the Baghdad Bounce. The warning came from the extended bearish divergence in the RSI window as represented by an extended September 2006-February 2007 resistance line.

A straight failure below the 200 day moving average is a sell signal even at the best of times, but the way that Yell delivered its failure by a massive gap to the downside showed that sentiment towards this company had collapsed. It is because of the gap that we know many were caught out. The low point as of the end of 2010 is the share price approaching 10p and plenty of debt issues to be addressed.

34. HMV (HMV): Hoarse Master's Voice February 2006

The digital revolution as far as music and video purchase and piracy has been one of the phenomena of the past decade. A company that has made sure whether by accident or design that it is always a step behind the flow of events has been music/books retailer HMV. A good example was the purchase of Waterstone's , which arguably added another dying business model to the existing one, and at top dollar. The icing on the cake as far as the bears were concerned was the rejection of a takeover offer from private equity group Permeira of 190p a share. This was rejected, presumably on the basis that £0.75bn was too little, but not as little as the current market capitalisation around the £120m mark – the Fred Goodwin Award For Business Acumen is in the post to all concerned parties.

On the charting front there was a typical set up to a bearish disaster for HMV shares from September 2005 when we were treated to the 50/200 day moving average dead cross accompanied by a gap to the downside meaning a 215p – 220p zone short entry. This took the stock quite directly to 180p by the end of October. But the real fun was in January/February 2006 with the island bottom reversal as the market was caught on the hop on two counts, firstly the Permeira bid and second the fact that it was only at 190p a share. What is noticeable is that throughout the "takeover" period the shares never came close to testing the 200 day moving average. The usual useful rule of three failures below the 200 day line being the trigger for an extended decline did pan out. By the end of 2010 HMV shares had continued their multiyear bear market to make it into the 30p's.

35. Carphone Warehouse (CPW): It Is Good To TalkTalk March 2010

It may be the case that everyone and their mother knew 25 years ago when the first yuppie brick mobile phones arrived and flash people had phones in the car that this was the way forward and the business to be in. But it was Charles Dunstone who took action at the end of the 1980s. By the beginning of the 2010s the largest independent mobile phone retailer in Europe – relatively unaffected by the economic crisis (we all need a phone) was in a position to simply keep on maximising shareholder value. In March 2010 the group hived off its internet services arm TalkTalk (TALK) with quite extraordinary results for the share price.

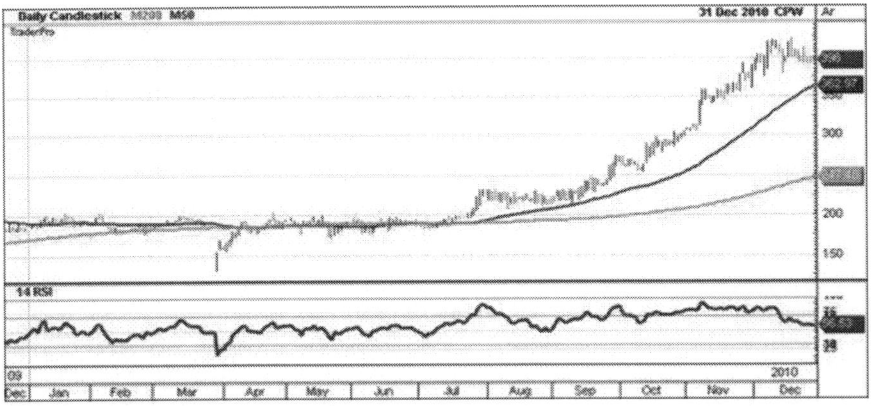

What happened on March 29th with the loss of TalkTalk was that Carphone shares were marked down to 135p on the open versus the previous close at 190p – a quite logical result given that a chunk of the business was off on a separate path. But it was the gap up for the shares on March 30th that delivered the big technical signal in that the previous day's price action was rendered an island day bottom – a massive buy signal. Only an end of day close back below the 155p gap low would upset the signal and this was not triggered. Indeed, the shares soared to 190p plus in a matter of days, filling the chart gap caused by the corporate split.

In fact, there was more in days and weeks to come in that July 27th saw a golden cross between the 50/200 day moving averages versus an end of day close at 216p as an entry point. By the end of the year, and with the golden cross still in force Carphone shares had hit 400p – a very good example of less being more. It is also a good example of a situation where there were rather generously, two opportunities to get on board a great breakout situation.

36. Smith & Nephew (SN.): Everything But The Bid November 2010

I hope that by the time this book is published Smith & Nephew is no longer an independent company. As a stock market performer it was dull, slightly accident prone, and extremely difficult to chart due to extended periods of limp price action. But things started to liven up for the medical devices company in the autumn of 2010 as takeover speculation bubbled up. Arguably, even this heightened state of activity was rather pedestrian as compared to the high octane action in the resources area of the stock market, but as I spotted S&N at the time and it is a particular favourite, here it is in *101 Charts*.

The criticism of S&N is that while the shares rarely offer a big or indeed a quick reward to traders, before even a modest move the price action is particular tough as far as the degree of difficulty. This was seen over the summer of 2010 as the stock was clearly base building, but from July to October delivered multiple bear traps in the 550p-570p zone. Therefore the November 5th gap to the upside was like a breath of fresh air in terms of being a straightforward technical opportunity. The deal at that point was to go long of the shares with an end of day close stop loss below the bottom of the gap at 559p. As things turned out there was nothing more to be done. December 8th delivered a gap through the 200 day moving average – a fresh buy signal which allowed the stop to be raised to the bottom of the second gap at 591p. The only thing missing by the end of the year was a bid approach, but for those in at the first gap buy signal such an issue was somewhat academic.

37. AIG (AIG): The Greatest Gap Fill Ever?

As well as being the greatest gap fill ever, I am wondering whether AIG is simply one of the best charting situations ever. Being bailed out meant that the group went from being Lehman Brothers mark II to the equivalent of being offered a Lamborghini for the price of a Mini. And it shows on the daily chart – not once but twice. Even more of a badge of greatness is that you didn't need to have the trading skills of a hedge fund manager to get on board March 2009's five session ride from $7 to $40. The first buy trigger was positive RSI divergence between February/March lows – with the added plus being the way that there were several days to contemplate going long. The second buy trigger was the gap higher on March 16th at $12.19 – an entry point for aggressive traders, with even slow coach buyers able to get on board the following day under $20 to double their money in 48 hours.

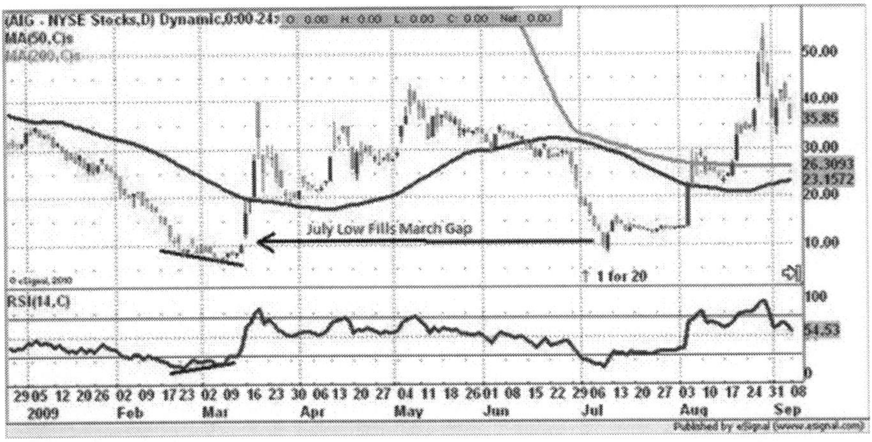

But great though this was, we were looking at only the first act of the great AIG charting experience of H1 2009. The key here was the opportunity for those who had missed the first opportunity to go long with a clear cut buy entry by placing a limit order at the floor of the unfilled gap of March 13th at $8.40 – buying at such charting points is an established rule. The result was that the intraday low of July 10th came in at $8.22 before the eventual near term peak came in at over $50 before the end of the following month.

AIG is therefore an example of how the results of the Credit Crunch were both as negative as one might have expected, but also positive in an almost unimaginable way too.

38. Polly Peck (POLY): The Man From Del Monte Says No

Given the way that the former CEO of former FTSE 100 conglomerate Polly Peck is currently back in the UK to face charges over the collapse of his company after a period of 20 years in exile in Northern Cyprus, it is probably not wise to take a punt as to what the final result and reputation of Asil Nadir will be. What would be a coup is if he did clear his name, although those who lost their investment in Polly Peck may not agree.

Polly Peck appears not only as a result of my fascination with the more colourful side of the City, but also because soon after a company comes off the stock market its chart is very difficult to get hold of and this was one I wanted to share.

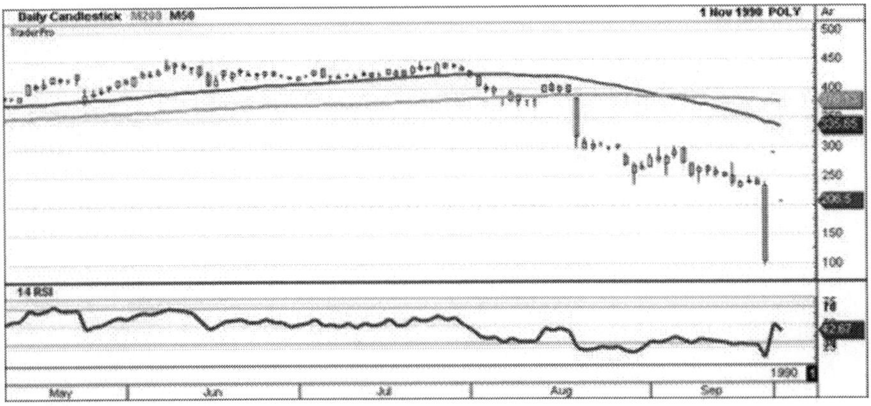

Polly Peck is a charting gift on the basis that the end came off the back of an island top above the 200 day moving average giving a sell opportunity from an opening price of 382p on August 17th 1990 to 316p on the close. The exact level of entry was somewhat academic as the decline from 300p to the suspension at the end of September was a relative clean affair.

EVERYDAY CHARTING: BREAD & BUTTER SET UPS/PERCENTAGE TRADES

It could very well be that those who are not seasoned campaigners as far as the stock market is concerned get the impression that opportunities only arrive when there are big events in the financial markets as a whole, or for the companies in question. This is not the case, indeed it can be argued that the most straightforward chances to make money from stocks are during "peace time" when there is relatively little newsflow and the price action is not confused by spurious speculation.

Something to remember regarding these examples, which are effectively a collection of favoured charting techniques that you have a choice of entering as soon as you see the setup, or waiting until an end of day close of the day the set up appears, or even the open of the day after – depending on how aggressive your strategy is.

But just as important is risk management. No signal is infallible, and the key to how successful you are in the stock market will be how you react to the 1/10 or 1/100 trade that could take you out of the game. Of course, you do not know which is the signal that could take you long of RBS (RBS) just before a 200p move to the downside, so you have to treat every one as if it could be toxic.

Price Trendline Breaks – Upside

Although trendlines can be dangerously subjective and hence have not been emphasized at all in this book, sometimes where to place a trendline is so obvious – usually alongside a moving average, that great rewards can be reaped. It can also help that after the downtrend line break a new uptrend line effectively acts as a trailing stop loss helping technical traders and investors to run their positions as long as possible.

39. Burberry (BRBY): Taking The Chequered Flag

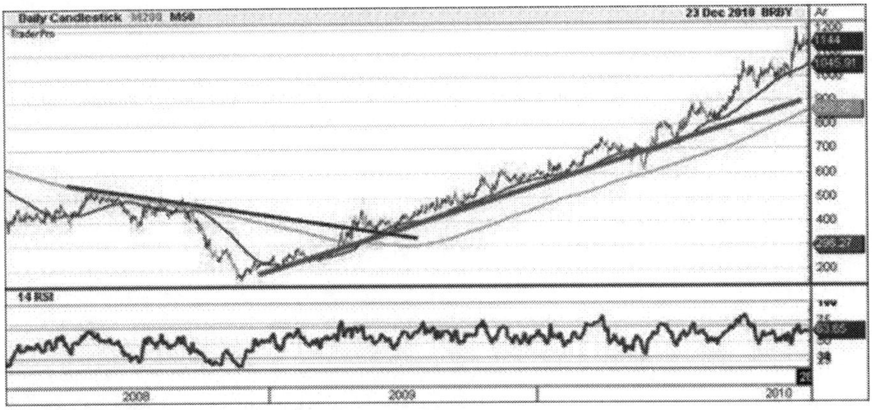

While the stock market's unquestioned love of Burberry continues to baffle, there was little difficulty in spotting a change of trend for the stock in April 2009 with the break of the 200 day moving average at the start of the month, and the May 2008 resistance line at no worse than 400p at the end of the month. Even though the green uptrend line was finally lost in May 2010 there was more than 200p on offer of upside from a very basic charting method. Using the 200 day moving average as a weekly close stop loss would have offered a journey through 1,000p.

Price Trendline Breaks – Downside

40. Game Group (GMG): A Christmas Collapse

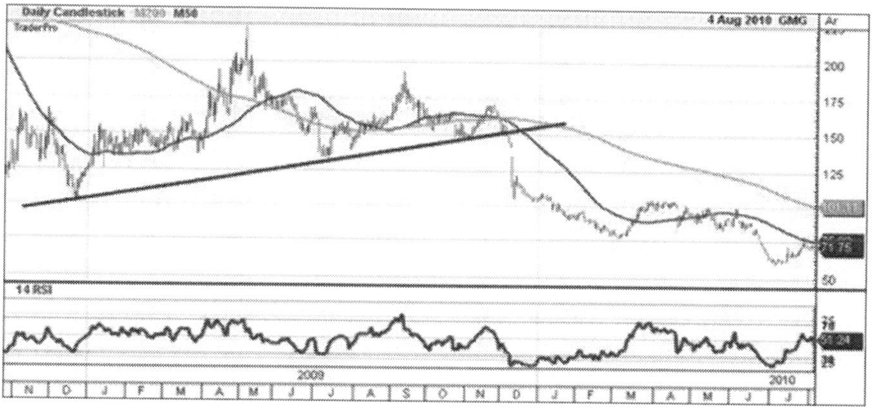

I suppose the fundamental issue with computer games software retailer Game Group is that it shares with HMV (HMV) a basic problem with the business model in terms of the delivery of the products it deals with. In charting terms it can be seen how drawing a trendline here through 2009 support could have acted as an early warning on a new leg down for the shares – ideally ahead of the December 2009 gap down. Of course, the plus point here is that even if you had not drawn the line, selling out or going short in the wake of the gap or 50/200 day moving average sell cross were other valid technical triggers ahead of the stock nearly halving in three months.

RSI Trendline Breaks – Upside

41. Shire Pharma (SHP): The First Signal On M&A?

While RSI trendlines are no big secret in technical analysis I do feel they are under used and unloved, particularly with relation to how effective they can be. In choosing Shire Pharma we have not only a great example of a RSI trendline break, but also an excuse to cover a company which would be an ideal takeover candidate – at least from the opinion of someone with all the experience of the drugs sector that one can have when both parents are medical doctors.

This opportunity in Shire from March 2009 is a standout on the basis that it could have been drawn in February, was then tested twice in March before the third successful break on March 31st as the stock gapped up, In fact, one could have traded this situation only on the gaps, but the RSI trendline break provided not only a backup signal, but also a measure of the power behind the eventual move to the upside.

RSI Trendline Breaks – Downside

42. BAE Systems (BA.)

From my perspective quibbling over the business practices of defence contractor BAE Systems (BA.) is about as useful as urging participants of the Battle of the Somme to wear an extra vest lest they catch a chill. However, I am not going to take this up with either the Serious Fraud Office or the Department of Justice as they are bigger than me. They were also apparently bigger than BAE and it coughed up a fine which could be regarded as a windfall tax, and subsequently went on with its business.

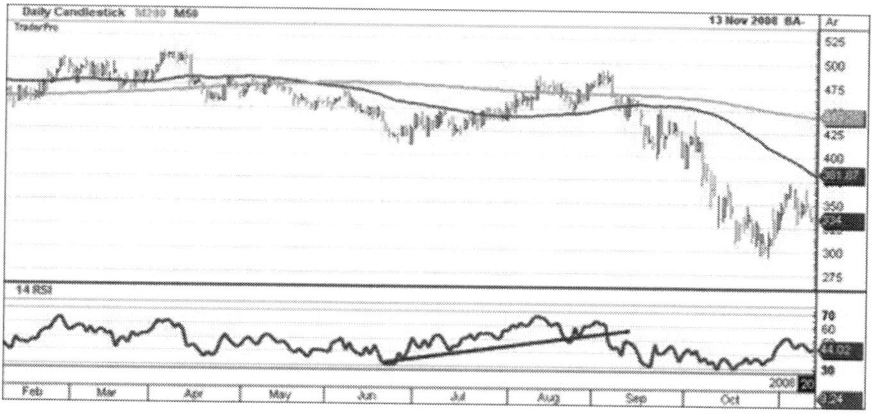

The run up to the investigation and slap on the wrist was reflected on the daily chart of BAE via a June 2009 RSI trendline break in early September – the failure coming on the third test of the line after it could have been drawn for the first time. If nothing else it provided a great short entry above 450p (prior to a sub 300p low) after the double death trap above the 200 day moving average in August/September – the aftermath of the 50/200 day moving average sell cross in June.

My suggestion is that for stocks that traders follow have RSI trendlines maintained on a continuous basis as a method of identifying turning points ahead of price movement.

Support Above Old Resistance

43. Aggreko (AGK): Technical Power Surge

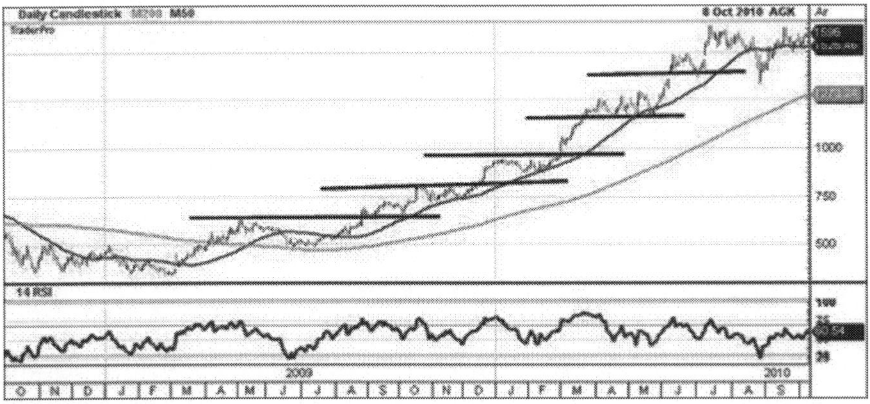

I do not think I have seen any other charting book emphasise enough what is perhaps the most simple technical rule of them all, support coming in at or above old resistance. This is a phenomenon only seen in the strongest of situations, with the added bonus being that it is possibly the best cure against "the trade that got away." In other words, looking upon the Aggreko daily chart in H1 2009 you might have thought it was too late to go long 200p-300p off the lows made by the temporary power group. But from October the shares started putting in new support at and above previous highs and therefore buying in at 700p, 800p or more was fair game. Even if you were unconvinced by this positive price action there was the 50 day moving average holding the shares up almost continuously from July 2009-August 2010.

Resistance Below Old Support

44. French Connection (FCCN): Falling FCUK

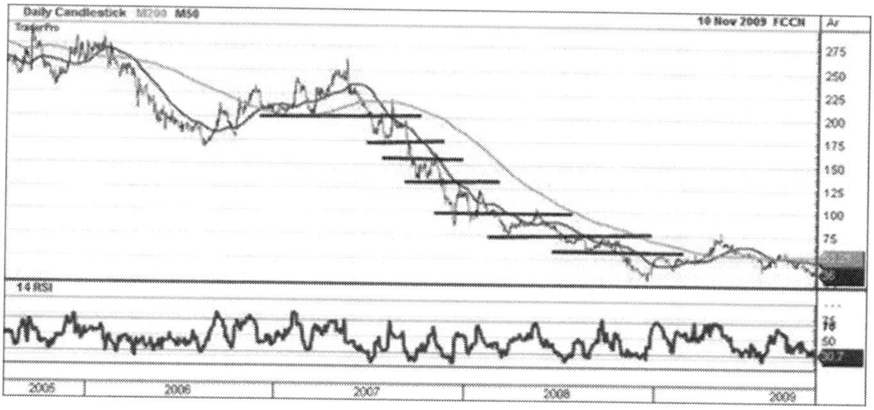

The marketing angle for French Connection was admittedly great at the time, but by the second half of the last decade wore rather thin as people presumably became rather less squeamish about using the underlying expletive. From a charting perspective it can be seen how as in the case of many of the Bread & Butter examples the evidence for the sell in this stock worked in more than one technical way. Indeed, we were flagged to the start of the breakdown here as early as February 2006 nearly the 250p level in the wake of a dead cross between the 50/200 day moving averages. Once short from this signal there was no real impetus to cover the position.

However, the sell message was reiterated by another dead cross in July 2007 of such power that the pattern of new resistance coming in at and below former support lasted for the best part of 18 months. The usual set up here is that the first time there is a failure at or below former support short entries can be taken for extended periods.

Bear Traps

Given the way we are told that 90% or more of short term traders lose money, it would always be great to know when this has happened so that you can go in after they have lost. Through charting this somewhat remote sounding possibility stems from looking out for bull and bear traps. These can be described as temporary breaks of support at either end of the trading range. They are normally failed continuation or breakout attempts, and while they may appear sinister are merely the result of the ongoing battle between buyers and sellers.

45. Fresnillo (FRES): Multiple Minor Bear Traps

For Fresnillo, the silver miner, we have an example of multiple minor bear traps over an extended period. The traps come as initial lows in August, September, October and November and January are narrowly broken. Of course, one would expect these initial lows to be broken enough so that those buying the first low are stopped out before seeing the stock heading up in precisely the way they would have wished. There are two options here. First for such injured parties to run off in a sulk after the first losing trade, or second, use an end of day close back above the first intraday low as a fresh buy signal. In the case of the January intraday low of 656p it was broken down to 647p on February 5th, but an end of day close back above the old January support the same day – at 669p was a fresh buy signal and was not challenged prior to the new leg higher for the rally beginning.

Bull Trap

46. BG (BG.): A Lot Of Bull

If everyday examples of bread and butter opportunities means nasty, then BG is right on the mark. In the section of the BG daily chart we see how determined the shares seemed to be to get traders going long ahead of the October plunge from 1,200p to below 700p. Of course, you could turn the perspective on its head by suggesting that traders were trying and failing to get the shares to maintain the 200 day moving average through which there was a final bull trap at the end of September. However, this was not all a lost cause. The bearish divergence in the RSI window during both May and September indicated whether one should be looking to press the buy button or not. Even more helpful was the September 25th gap fill end of day close at 1,129p which finally ended BG's bull trap spree.

47. Gap Up, Buy - WPP (WPP)

Charting gaps are perhaps one of the most useful and clear cut forms of technical signal and the most practical in that the market itself "tells you" where your stop loss/profit target should be. They are also features who effectively underline the price action, rather in the way that exclamation marks work in language. In the case of WPP we can see how on no less than four occasions (two in July, one in September and one in October) the rebounds in the stock from both the 200 day and 50 day moving averages was punctuated by gaps to the upside. Helping us throughout the period was the way that the trend was indicated by the rising moving averages. Even better, anyone buying in the wake of the gap would never have had the normal stop loss – an end of day close for the share price back below the gap, threatened.

48. Gap Down, Sell – Sage (SGE)

One of the big pluses of gaps is that they can be the icing on the cake in terms of a charting set up which is well founded, but which some may still be holding back on pressing the "buy/sell" button. In the case of Sage in July 2004, the balance was certainly tipped in favour of the bears given the multiple failures for the shares just above the 200 day moving average, with the latest trigger for shorting being a bull trap in June through 185p. However, it was only with the gap down at the beginning of July below the 50 day moving average that we were tipped in favour of a strong sell on the basis that a five month range/consolidation between 165p and 185p was likely to end. Indeed, from the time of the gap down the 50 day moving average started to fall and this along with the 200 day line slipping shortly after was more than enough to deliver a range break to the downside.

49. Gap Fills – Aviva

The start of 2009 saw several gap opportunities, providing decent clear cut signals in both directions. Indeed, it is surprising to see so many gaps within such a relatively small period of time on the daily chart of a leading blue chip stock. The start of February saw unfilled gaps to the upside and downside where stop losses back below/above them respectively would not have been compromised. But it is the late February/March gap downs who provide the most "delicious" signals. This is said on the basis of the almost exactly fill of the gap tops the stock made just after the dip to the downside. As far as the February 27th move the gap top at 286.5p was filled on March 5th with a day high of 288.75p followed by a decline of over 100p the same session. Orders to sell at 286p or better would followed no more than the standard practice for such set ups. The March 23rd-March 24th island top (gap up and gap down) had a formation low of 245p, with the overlap to 249p, before another sharp drop for Aviva. Indeed, this period for the shares illustrates the way that it is perfectly possible to base a trading strategy wholly on a search for and play on these price action events.

50. The Exhaustion Gap - Royal Dutch Shell (RDSB)

While it has to be conceded that an exhaustion gap only reveals itself as having been the top/bottom of an extended move well after the event, there is still plenty of trading mileage in these wide open spaces of untraded prices. In the case of Shell it can be seen how the July gap to the upside may have gone relatively unnoticed if it were not for end of day close at 1,667p, back above the intraday low of May at 1,661p. The logical stop loss could have been as tight as an end of day close back below 1,661p – in the event of an unexpected reversal or market volatility. This provided the kind of "double" signal which has an extra degree of reliability. Indeed, the result here was that there was an eventual push back towards the main 200 day moving average resistance at 1,777p, essentially meaning that the gap/trap combo delivered the goods on the upside despite the post April sell off.

Payoff

As suggested with the example of Aviva, the bread and butter concept of technical/charting signals is one which has plenty of mileage and given how broad based it is means that you could be someone who only trades after gaps, or bear traps, RSI/trendline breaks. What helps these days is that increasingly trading software is so sophisticated it is possible to data trawl automatically for the set ups in question.

CHARTING CHALLENGES: THE FALKLANDS FAD FACTOR

Perhaps the best excuse to cover a couple of the Falkland Islands stocks, but have a decent reason for doing so long after they stop being the fad of the month, is to include them in a category almost all of their own as an example of a stock market mania . Indeed, the Falkland Factor could just as easily be any other fad in the market in charting terms, such as dot-com or software, green energy, precious metals, petroleum, tulips or railroads.

The reason behind this category is to underline the way that while the impression given in many of the examples in *101 Charts* could be that trading success is as easy as falling off a log, this is unfortunately not the case.

Of course, the best solution to this problem is to concentrate on "simple" percentage trade set ups of which we have many examples. But there is much to be learned by "stress testing" your approach on the most unpredictable and arguably impossible situations. As far as the Falkland oil & gas explorers were concerned the main problem was mixed success in finding any hydrocarbons, with often contradictory updates within a space of days.

51. Desire Petroleum (DES): Here A Gap, There A Gap

The Set Up

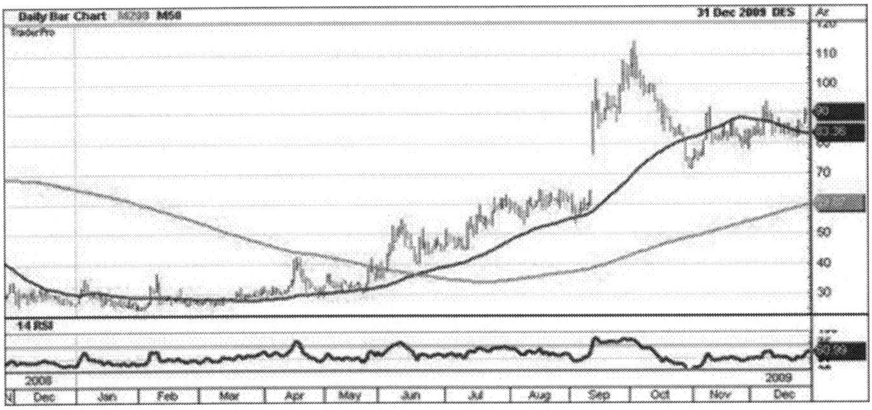

Cynics might argue that given the benefit of hindsight you can rationalise any chart in terms of notional buy and sell points. However, even this method might find trouble with the behaviour of Desire Petroleum in 2010, which was a rather sharp contrast to the saucer bottom acceleration to the upside seen in 2009 shown above. While we may expect difficult behaviour from a small cap oil & gas sector play, here it could be said that both fundamental and technical traders were taken to the limit.

Indeed, to describe Desire as being a prime example of a leap of faith play seems to fit the bill best. Part of the volatility issue here was intense private investor interest in a relatively small company, with the remainder being the obvious difficulties in exploring one of the more remote and speculative hydrocarbon prospects in the world.

The Outcome

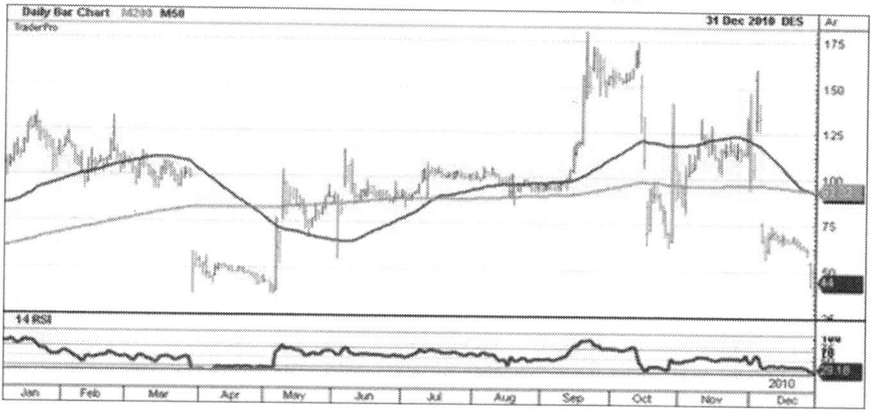

For the year of 2010 it is probably best to look at the most simple/straightforward charting events first. For instance, there was little to quibble about regarding the 50/200 day moving average buy cross following a saucer bottom going into the start of 2009. Unfortunately, it may have been the case that the relatively smooth ride in that year from below 30p to over 110p lulled traders into a false sense of security regarding how easy it is to make money from this stock. Indeed, once again the markets underline that after a straightforward move the payback can be severe, like ARM (ARM) in 2000. In the case of Desire it is difficult to imagine how the ride could have been any worse, the on/off nature of the oil prospecting success notwithstanding.

Hit number one was the March 29th gap down – not only a 50% one day decline but also a gap through the 200 day moving average. On the face of it this gap should have been the death knell for the bulls for the longest time and even permanently. This is especially the case given that it completed a rolling island top which the stock fell away from until a May 6th bear trap rebound below the March intraday low. While this may have been attainable, it required nerves of steel and a vast stop loss to get the better of.

Fortunately, the gap higher on May 10th through the 50 day moving average created an April/May island bottom with a gap fill buy opportunity at 69p. From this point only an end of day close below 69p would have been an exit signal (if you could handle the intraday dip to 55p on June 2nd. In fact the journey higher improved from July 15th with a 50/200 day moving average golden cross. This delivered a two month slow burn rally towards the 160p plus resistance of the year in October and that is when the charting fun (more precisely horror) began. Two gaps down in three sessions (October 13th and 15th) signalled a massive bear signal – especially through the 200 day moving averages.

The shares should have stayed down. Instead this situation turned into the most aggressive form of a trading range imaginable in the sense that the turning points were mapped out by gaps. This aggressive behaviour fitted in with what can sometimes be seen either side of the 200 day moving average, but knowing this still did not make Desire an easy play. The final sting in the tail was that the top of the October gap at 161.25p remained unfilled by 1.25p on December 2nd probably denying most bears intending to sell the top of the range. Going forward it will be interesting to see how Desire shares can once again deny the December double unfilled gap down when combined with a 50/200 day moving average dead cross – unless it finds a decent oil filled prospect.

Payoff

Desire is a great example of a stock that traders should be avoiding, but one where the punting addiction for many would make it almost impossible to resist. While there were great trading rewards to be made over a two year period, bolt from the blue bad news would have probably meant that many would have had more than their fingers burnt. Put simply, a stock that can rise or fall 50% overnight is probably not the best to be jobbing in and out of on a regular basis.

52. Rockhopper: Jumpin' Jumpin'

The Set Up

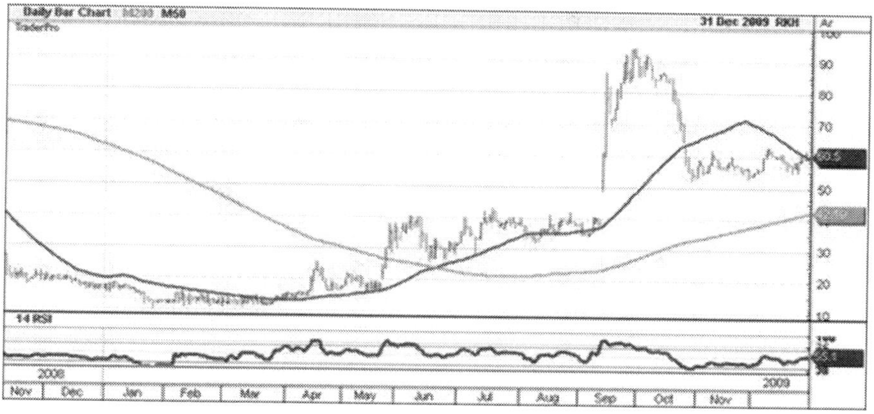

There is nothing in the stock market that gives so much joy to so many as the journey which leads to a share price "ten bagging". In fact, in the space of less than 24 months the Rockhopper delivered a range of 10.75p to 549p. Of course, the motivation was the smell of hydrocarbons , some of it real and some imaginary. Helping the likes of Rockhopper along on the upside is the knowledge that tiddlers from the middle of the last decade, such as Tullow Oil (TLW) and Cairn Energy (CNE) are now fully paid up members of the FTSE 100.

The years 2009-2010 were key in terms of the charting history of Rockhopper. The point to note here are the types of technical formations shareholders were treated to, and compare and contrast them with the best of the other hot stocks of the recent past.

The Outcome

The rise of Rockhopper was initiated by a saucer bottom from November 2008 – June 2009. Unfortunately, it is hard to be a fan of a reversal formation where you normally only realise what is going on once the bulk of the move has occurred. Relapses can also be exceptionally painful from saucers. Instead, a bear trap rebound accompanied by bullish divergence through the 50 day moving average then at 12p (a 13p entry) on March 26th 2009 was the clear entry point – if you were watching for it.

If you were not, a scan of end of day closes above the 200 day moving average (using Updata) would have delivered a 28.5p entry on May 26th. The usual rule is that three successful tests for support wholly above the 200 day moving average (ideally the moving average is rising) should lead to substantial gains – equivalent to what is seen in ten bagger stocks. (RBS, many financials and indices in 2008 illustrated what happens when there are multiple failures below the 200 day line.)

The final week of July saw the 200 day line start to rise, with August and the first week of September seeing successful tests for support prior to the big September 10th gap up day through to 58.5p. At least on the basis that the stock hit a September 94.5p before pulling back – on this basis Rockhopper was kind, arguably too kind to the bulls, especially those who had come to the situation late.

The following eight months added fuel to the theory that markets enjoy doling out a painful revenge if they have been inadvertently generous on any given move. The two thirds decline back to 31p in April 2010 can only be classed as one of the more painful countermove/bear trap events of the recent past. This is because the shares flipped from what could be described as maximum bull status to maximum bearishness.

Perhaps not too surprisingly this happened in a gradual fashion as the stock lost the momentum it had found above the 200 day moving average. Indeed, it was the loss of this feature under the falling 10 day moving average on March 9th that warned a problem was on its way for the bulls, just as losing the 10 day moving average at 90p at the beginning of October had been a nudge to take profits at that time. In fact, there was a clear three time failure in the 60p 200 day moving average zone prior to the second test of the sub 40p zone before the massive turn on a dime rebound came.

If there was ever an illustration of how some stocks are only for the seasoned professional, this was it. This is despite the way that the fundamental trigger for the turnaround was the revelation by Rockhopper that it had made a high quality oil find in the Falklands. Technically the task here was to buy the end of day close above the 200 day line when the shares were at 93.5p. Clearly, with no obvious stop loss other than an end of day close back below the 200 day line zone then at 55p, this was not a purchase for everyone. But at least what the May/June gaps higher did prove successfully is that second time around through the 200 day line Rockhopper was not going to let traders down.

Payoff

Resources stocks are not for widows/orphans even at the best of times. If you want normality chose the staid Royal Dutch Shell (RDSB), although even it can deliver a painful googly on occasion. With Rockhopper it was perfectly possible to be short and caught out by the May 6th 2010 surge, with no significant technical warning. The only salvation was that of a stop loss which could have been placed just above the ten day or 50 day moving averages if you were unfortunate enough to have been short of the stock.

The reality is that Rockhopper has been chosen as the worst example of volatility and it suits such a role very well. This is shown in the subsequent June 4th gap and the September/October and December 2nd – December 3rd island tops. Presumably those who consciously get involved with stocks and markets that behave in such a fashion accept the attendant risks and rewards.

53. A Year In The Life: Autonomy – Nice Tech Stock, Shame About The Financial PR 2010

One of the great faults of those writing about the business of predicting the financial markets is that the impression is given of everything being sweetness and light. The stock brokers give you the buy for the long term spiel and the doomsters of late go for end of the world scenario that can apparently absorb the type of 50% rally seen in the FTSE 100 between March-September 2009 and/or the Dow's best September for a lifetime during 2010. The reality is that few opportunities are easy, either because they are simply well discussed or because the greatest technical signals occur at totally counterintuitive times. This is what we want in terms of going against the herd, but the hard truth of all markets be they stocks, bond or houses is that most people buy at the top and sell at the bottom. If is very difficult to do anything else. I liked the words of a US market commentator when he said that most of us are hotwired to lose money on the markets. The idea behind charting is that it forces us to ignore these instincts.

Nevertheless, I do not want to give the impression that with charting making money is a one way ticket. To illustrate this I am running through a couple of the nastiest stocks I could find in terms of not only the price action, but the interaction between price and newsflow.

The Set Up

For the past ten years Autonomy has been one of the UK's brightest tech sector hopes, a point underlined by the way that after being blasted out of the FTSE 100 in March 2001, it was promoted once again in 2008. In fact, it may have spent more of the last decade in the blue chip category if people actually understood what it does. My understanding is simply that it is a knowledge management software company, and I really do not want to know any more. At a guess though, the reason for the volatility of the shares during 2010 was a function of both the company hitting a critical phase of its development as well as a curious set of events and misunderstandings. This is not the place to go into too much detail, but suffice to say that from mid-2010 to the end of the year most times the company made a significant announcement the shares dropped 10% or more.

Outcome

February 3rd 2010 saw a textbook set of excellent results for Q4 with full year revenues up 47% and full year profit from operations up 59%. So far, so good in the sense that there was some initial profit taking via a gap down on February 10th providing a buy opportunity on March 3rd when there was an end of day close back above it. In fact, with all the price action in H1 2010 at or well above the 200 day moving average the message here was to buy on dips or continuation signals.

The build-up to the Q1 2010 update was a solid one in share price terms, and therefore it was perhaps only to be expected that there could be a sell off after news of a revenues rise of 50% and a profit from operations surge of 48%. This was essentially what happened, with technical traders helped out by a gap down on April 28th opening at 1,804p taking the shares below 1,700p by May 10th. Indeed, May/June delivered a series of quite appealing gap entry and exit signals as it was clear that the market was trying to balance the view that Autonomy was hitting a near fundamental peak versus the idea that this is a long term growth situation.

The balance started to swing in favour of those who judged the good news to be in the price by the time of the Q2 update on July 22nd where revenue growth was "only" 28% and adjusted net profit up 32%. Clearly by this time fundamental traders were getting a sinking feeling. From a technical perspective there were two standouts. The first was the relatively straightforward sell signal of the gap down on the day of the Q2 announcement leaving you to remain short while there was no end of day close back above the gap at 1,801p. (You could have jumped the gun with a gap fill sell signal on July 20th above 1,800p.) Those who did not fancy a 100p stop loss could have gone for an equally valid stop loss as an end of day close back above the gap bottom at 1,700p or even have gone short on the August 8th gap down.

We were flipped back on the long side on September 2nd via a gap higher to deliver the right side of an island bottom, and 150p of upside during the rest of the month. But it can be said quite fairly that the start of October saw things turning nasty both on a technical and fundamental front. The first trading day of the month delivered a September 22nd gap fill buy signal, one which proved to be valid for only the next two sessions before an October 6th warning on the company's full year revenue consensus by 3%. The shares fell by 20%. There are two points to be made, firstly it was just as well the revenue call was only lowered by 3%, second, why did the group even bother to mention such a small change – one that could easily be within acceptable margins of error?

Whatever the fundamental realities of this shooting in the foot event, from my perspective this was one of the most brutal examples of an unpredictable event – especially as it was not a scheduled update, or went with the charting flow, or was objectively that much of a disaster. True, it is possible to fumble for a charting double top/bearish divergence in the RSI window, going into the 20% dive this was no worse than a wait and see for the longs, rather than a get out at all costs.

The situation was redeemed to some extent off the back of a bear trap rebound/bullish RSI divergence buy signal on the November 26th close back above October's 1,319p intraday low, and a December 13th gap higher by signal up to 1,410p. However, it is likely that for most traders Autonomy has been struck off their Christmas card list for quite some time to come.

Payoff

It is quite ironic and just plain surprising that one of the most unpredictable events in *101 Charts* comes from a slight revenue downgrade by a tech company, even more than geopolitical trauma of economic disaster, but this appears to be the case with Autonomy. Nevertheless, the October 2010 incident does serve to remind us that even at the best of times the charting approach cannot spot every event before it happens, even if at times it can appear to have magical powers.

54. A Year In The Life: PartyGaming – Bwinning And Losing

The Set Up

One of the problems that those who are drawn to the financial markets have is that they are naturally gamblers. This is not glamorous as the word gambler could very easily be substituted for the word losers, when the goal idea is to be an investor. The charting methodology is a framework to offset this issue, especially as one result of the gambling affliction is for those who suffer from it to be most interested in the most volatile and difficult markets. This will tend to mean mining/commodities stocks, or simply the most volatile, where there is the greatest volatility and as a consequence the greatest chance of losing money. I will sidestep the Freudian interpretation of why men (yes, women do not suffer death wish affliction in general) and simply mention that I do have an unhealthy interest in volatile shares.

PartyGaming, the online gaming group has been one of the most "active" of plays, and as a broker friend of mine once said, PartyMaiming, is very often the result for short term traders here. The lead up to and immediately after its proposed merger with Bwin reveals lessons not only as far as how to play the most volatile stocks, but also is a "stress test" as far as how to handle difficult set ups and situations as a whole.

Outcome

It seems to me that while the purpose of writing a book on the financial markets may be to impart knowledge to others in a (nearly) philanthropic fashion, one of the side effects is that the author is forced to learn more about the subject in question. Revisiting PartyGaming's chart of 2010 the technicals actually appear rather tame even though the stock is included here as an example of horror. It was, unless you were able to look at it in an objective, charting manner. This would be perfectly easy for the Spock character in the original Star Trek TV series, but unless you are half Vulcan/possess pointy ears and employ only logic in your approach to the markets, there can be a mountain of discipline to climb.

2010 on the PartyGaming chart started in classic and straightforward fashion. There was a golden cross between the 50/200 day moving averages on January 26th. I would not class this as a fantastic opportunity as those who hurled themselves long in the wake of the signal entered at 290p and more and had to take a retracement back to 270p. But those familiar with the stock will be aware that stop losses of 20p-40p are common place. An end of day close back below an exhaustion gap of 326p delivered a sell signal versus the 339p March intraday high offering a modest fall to 310.5p a week later. But this was easily bettered by a fresh gap down sell signal through the 50 day moving average just above 300p. In six sessions there was a decline to sub 260p from a 300p plus short entry.

After this however, we were looking at a rather more rocky ride, albeit one that was dominated by a May 25th gap below the 200 day moving average, and a failure at the 200 day moving average on June 16th. My involvement with the shares came with a dare devil buy recommendation at 238p on July 9th after the July 6th gap higher. This appeared to be a great call, and one where the suggested stop loss of 209p was too wide. It was, but just by 3.5p. Indeed, the countermove retracement of July 22nd was typical of this stock's mysterious ability to flush out traders before the best rallies.

The bear flush out came on July 29th with the spike to 333p in the wake of a proposed merger with Austrian counterpart Bwin. This could/should have been the end of the charting story, and for this reason it seemed perfectly acceptable to take your eye off the ball as far as the August 4th gap down for the shares which suggested a possible 300p plus entry point. The shares hit 252p before the end of the month without any stress for the bears, unless of course they were concerned that there could have been another M&A deal on the table – enough to scare out the bulk of fundamental trading contenders.

The main interest for the rest of the year came from the interaction of the stock with the 50 and 200 day moving averages, as well as the fact that even though the merger had been struck the shares were just as volatile as ever. The June 16th 200 day moving average failure was repeated almost exactly by an October 27th failure at the same feature, an event (with an end of day close stop loss back above the 200 day line) that led to a near vertical decline for the stock going into November. The 50 day line did the honours as the resistance zone for the December bear run.

Payoff

PartyGaming illustrates very well how greed may get traders into technical set ups – despite fear of volatility and "surprise" events, but that fear may just as easily keep them out of the game. After the Bwin merger it seemed logical to assume that the case was closed as far as trading PartyGaming, but as can be seen from the daily chart, if anything there were more opportunities provided both by gaps initially and then via moving average reactions. While that broker cliché that you have to be in it to win it may not sound anything more than a glib sales pitch, in this instance it does appear appropriate.

IPO - OLOGY

The period in the immediate aftermath of the financial sector crisis of 2007-8 was obviously not going to be a great one for companies raising cash on the stock market. However, once it became clear that firstly it was not a great idea to ask the banks for cash, and that with a deposit rate of less than 0.5% retail and institutional investors who had not been blasted by the bear market in equities were very keen to get a decent return above inflation, the idea of an IPO could be a good one. In fact, the key to the revival in IPOs may be the desperation on the part of some to achieve the largest returns possible in what is still a very troubled economic environment.

55. Betfair (BET): A Sell At The Open

The Set Up

I have to admit that I was swayed against online betting group Betfair from the start, as I really could not do the math as to how this company, which does not appear to have any great difference to any other of its sector members, could have a valuation of £1bn plus. Of course, part of the dislike could be jealousy, enhanced by the £250m plus raised by leading shareholders when the company came to market. While this was not necessarily a sell signal, it was not a vote of confidence in the price tag either.

But while I recommended a sell bet on the shares at 1,540p soon after the group came to market and then suggested a quick exit less than 100p of profit later, there were those in the City who had more forthright views. Forthright enough to deliver what in my opinion was the best broker note I have ever read, if only in terms of the entertainment value. In fact, it is the City equivalent of the Virgin Airline complaint letter.

Paul Leyland at Investec delivered a 445p target on a stock then valued at £13 and clearly meant it to go down to the suggested level. A particular highlight as far as the ouch factor was the comment that Betfair's financial market trading spin off was a "solution without a problem." If only all such research was so incisive, and more importantly, correct.

The Outcome

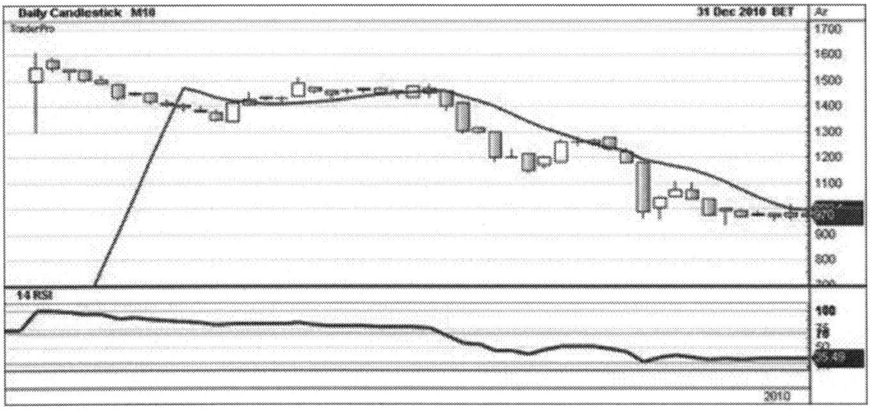

As described above, it was not difficult to miss Betfair as a fundamental sell on the open, even if you have not been reading the Evil Knievil Diaries for years and acquired a sense of the big man's hubris detector when it comes to the corporate scene. As far as the best technical way of dealing with a new IPO, which could in the early stages see its share price fly around all over place, is usually to focus on the trading range of the first week. This combined with the start of the ten day moving average trace in what will usually be a fast moving search for the "correct" valuation. In the case of Betfair the first week trading range was 1,470p to 1,610p, with the following week delivering a break to the downside that triggered a punishing decline for the shares to the end of 2010. At no point was the opening high of 1,610p ever under threat.

Looking at the shares from the daily chart perspective, it is the gap down on October 29th that was key here. Not only was there a reasonable downside directly from this chart feature, but the usual charting rule to sell the top of a gap down – at 1,490p, worked perfectly on November 15th. Essentially, it was all downhill from here, although those who wanted to see clear weakness before going short could have waited for a failure below the ten day line either on November 26th or November 27th just to make sure.

In terms of the position by December, the way that new resistance was coming in well below former support on both the 10th and 16th implies that while sub 500p may seem rather pessimistic, so far there has been nothing in the price action to suggest that there could be significant downside even from present levels.

Payoff

Reading broker notes can sometimes be fun, and even correct. Now and again there is a significant difference between what a company's IPO price should have been and what powerful City institutions can achieve. This does leave opportunities on the downside even in a rising stock market.

56. Ocado (OCDO): A Profits Free Delivery

The exercise of floating has been an eye opener in how the City works. Apparently, even after all that has happened in the past few years it is still possible to fool all the people some of the time. Indeed, I would love to know who managed to get this company away and use their services. Perhaps with their skills I could be marketed as the world's leading chartist, or the next George Clooney, or a future Prime Minister? The financial press bemoaned some minor detail about Ocado not having made a profit or an equivalent firm going bust nearly ten years ago. My personal quibble is that Ocado's service is one that the major supermarkets could easily do or could have done themselves if there was money in it. But hats off to the founders of Ocado, you made money out of nothing, you were entrepreneurial, and that is what this country needs (Prime Minister type rhetoric).

Outcome

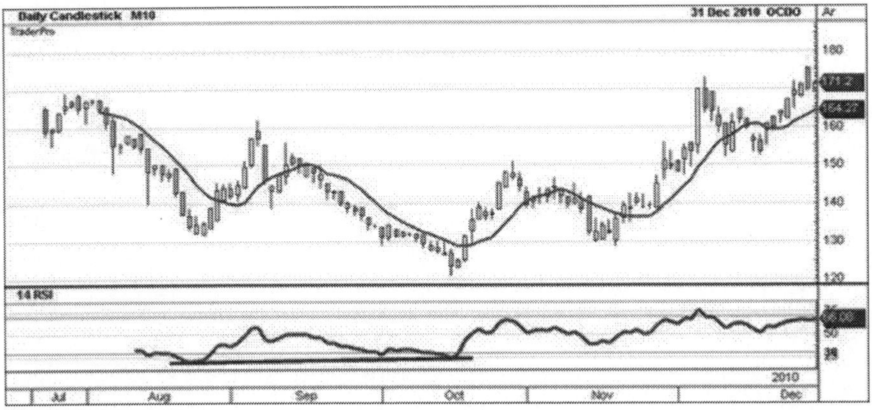

The financial media really got into trashing the IPO of the online grocer, with the 200p-275p range suggested by the group valuing it at £1bn. For some reason not having made a profit in ten years and being at the mercy of just one supplier which it is in competition with was seen as something to quibble about. Therefore it was actually quite an achievement that the shares opened at 180p, but not too much of a surprise that they tanked almost from the start. Following the opening weekly range idea – the support came in at 155p and resistance at 180p. This was broken in the third week to the downside and essentially the opening support became new resistance for the next three months.

Ironically, by mid-December it appeared that Ocado shares had been rehabilitated. This was off the back of what had effectively been a triple bottom reversal formation established near the 130p level over the autumn, after bullish RSI divergence was established between the August/October lows – the latter was lower. The resultant bear trap rebound lead to a three steps forward/two steps back rally with the key event being December support at 152p coming in a penny above the October intraday high. An end of day close above the top of a December 15th gap down was the buy signal for a retest of the best levels since the IPO.

Payoff

The initial trade in Ocado was a reflection of the ill will towards the company even before it came to market. But what has been interesting here is that the law of diminishing returns was evident for the bears and in a relatively short space of time the Ocado technicals were transformed even though on the face of it nothing of significance had changed on the fundamental front. The message is that it pays to keep an open mind in the early life of a stock's listing, as the market can take a schizophrenic approach to analysing a new group's prospects.

Trends can therefore turn on a dime, and with speed being the ultimate weapon for the market, if you doubt the wisdom of a position, it pays to exit first and ask questions after. The extremely bullish W shaped price pattern for Ocado up to the end of 2010 was certainly at odds with the initial contempt analysts and the financial media had for the company.

57. Supergroup (SGP): The Trendy Uptrend

The Set Up

Being someone in the prime of my middle age, at least in head of hair terms, the word supergroup always triggers in the mind the members of 1960's blues rock combo Cream – Eric Clapton, Jack Bruce and Ginger Baker. But as far as the stock market was concerned in 2010 there was a rather more up to date entity to chase, in the form of fashion retailer Supergroup (SGP). Given how out of touch I am this company just seemed to be say a French Connection mark II, with the brands such as Cult and SuperDry destined to become uncool within months rather than years. But such negative thinking would have missed out on a FTSE 250 stock tripling in a matter of months, so once again an open mind and technical analysis were the way forward.

Outcome

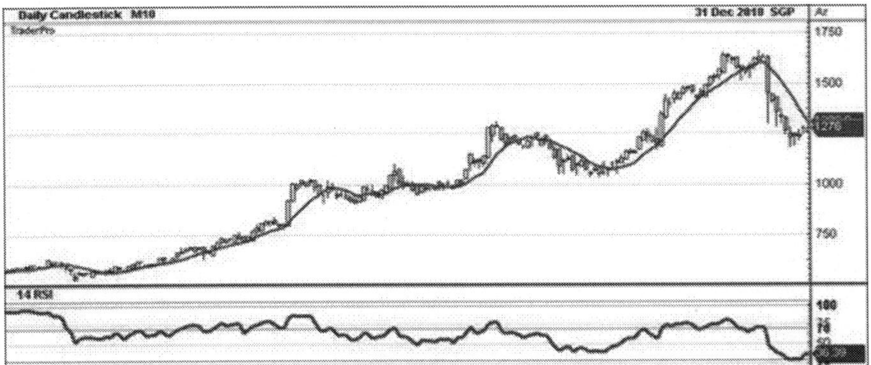

The opening weekly range for Supergroup was 499p-560p, and particularly wide. To add the challenge was the way that the second week started with a gap higher above this range, meaning that there was a risk of a stop loss of 61p plus being called on. Nevertheless, the equivalent of a £3 or £5 a penny buy bet or the equivalent would not have been too uncomfortable, especially as to this day it would not have been hit.

The initial push for Supergroup was to 630p, a decent profit for the opening week method. On the ten day moving average basis, with entry triggers as end of day closes above or below the line. The result of this was a buy on April 16th at 582p, a sell close on May 5th at 590p (after the 630p April 29th peak) and the big buy of May 19th at 575p which guided the stock to 943p on July 30th. Clearly, not all IPOs play ball like this, and of course Supergroup would not be appearing here if it were not for the exceptional move that was seen in H2 2010.

Payoff

Weekly range breaks only work well in markets that are trending or are expected to do so in a momentum fashion – such as commodities stocks and IPOs in the initial burst of stock market life. The same can be said of end of day closes above/below the ten day moving average – something which is embarrassingly easy given fast moving and free flowing price action. Ways of ensuring that you get on board such stocks be they IPOs or not are to seek out the most liquid/high volume situations and/or the most newsworthy.

58. Essar Energy (ESSR): Riding The Rollercoaster

The Set Up

There is always something special regarding an IPO which heads straight into the FTSE 100, especially as you know there is going to be plenty of share price action as tracker funds jockey for position. Added volatility is added by the way that India focused Essar is in the oil & gas sector. It gave traders extra reason for getting involved after reducing the float price to 420p from a 450p to 550p range.

Outcome

The 420p float price compared to the opening price of 415p, and opening week range of 358p to 415p. The range was broken in week 5 ending May 31st with a 435p close. The opening range low was never broken. The opening pattern was sell/buy /sell/buy, in other words stopping out the longs who bought in initially, then the shorts just above the initial weekly range, followed by a higher low at 380p on May 25th which the bulls may have missed out on, waiting for a better price. The alternative end of day close above/below the ten day moving average method delivered a sell on May 24th at 402p – a decline to 380p, and then a reverse to the long side on May 27th at 419p. From this 17p loss there was a rally to 475p at best, with a 454p close out and fresh short on July 7th. Following the ten day moving average approach would have resulted in a choppy but not unprofitable ride over subsequent weeks and months. 380p was tested once again in August to give the rally towards the end of the year.

Payoff

It would appear that going by the initial IPO weekly range and the ten day moving average provides a reasonable framework for the opening gambit in a cross section of recent IPOs, none of which could be classed by anyone as being easy to get a handle on. IPOs have the double difficulty of being extra fast moving and very often possessing extra price volatility due to the fundamental crosswinds provided by the financial media and the kneejerk/wrong analysis of City analysts trying to make a splash.

PROFIT WARNINGS

A search of UK profits warnings of the recent past on the Guardian.co.uk website will reveal that at least as far as that source of data is concerned 2008 was a big year for the genre with its summer of profits warnings. What is interesting is that while there is much intrigue as far as insider trading on possible bid approaches/takeovers, I have never heard of anyone being prosecuted on front running a profits warning. It would appear that if the general public do not understand something, the authorities are not that bothered. But for normal investors it is certainly the case that a profits warning, or even a series of such events is just about the worst thing that can happen. Therefore it would pay to use charting techniques in order to cut out of a position before the deadly announcement arrives. This is not always possible, as by definition having to make a warning can even catch the management of a company off guard as negative fundamental momentum gathers pace. The ideal scenario from the perspective of a trader is that they will already be short in the market beforehand, and a warning will be a pleasant surprise.

59. Marks & Spencer (MKS): Sales Slump Warning July 2nd 2008

The M&S profits warning of July 2008 was probably the perfect scenario for the bears given that technically the door they were pushing on had been in sell mode for a year. The loss of the 200 day moving average and the uptrend in the stock had come in during May 2007, with resistance coming in below this feature until a typical "death trap" with the price action moving narrowly above the 200 day moving average at the beginning of November 2007.

This is normally seen in the most bearish of situations (Lloyds Banking (LLOY) offered a death trap the previous month) and there was an accelerating decline for M&S from that point on. Just in case you missed the autumn 2007 message, January 2008 saw a double unfilled gap down. It would appear that the market had taken the warning that tough conditions could last for Middle England's grocer for up to two years to heart. Indeed, the double gap down not only implied an extended decline but also that there were doubts over the financial viability of the group itself.

Just in case there was anyone else not quite convinced of the idea that the July update could bring bad news there was a share price gap down on June 6th – one that remained unfilled going into the July 2nd announcement that lead to another 25% gap down. In fact, after this bear party the stock was kind enough to signal a buy opportunity via the July 17th gap up, an event that created an island bottom with the profits warning gap down. The message was that while above the bottom of the gap at 243p on an end of day close basis the shares were a buy. Although the gap was filled intraday, there was a rally to the 50 day moving average and the 300p level within a month. Indeed, this rally was the first indication that M&S had actually been too bearish with its early summer warning. After the obligatory bear trap/stop loss probing back below 200p in the autumn the stock began an extended recovery.

60. Rentokil (RTO): The Fourth Profits Warning July 25th 2008

A very good rule on the stock market is said to be that profits warnings come in threes, and therefore if nothing else one should resist the temptation to bottom fish after a major share price slump just on a kneejerk reaction to the stock appearing cheap. Pest control group Rentokil was very much the exception that proved the rule in the middle of the Credit Crunch bear market of 2008. It was also a company which was very much still under the curse of Sir Clive Thompson, who as Mr 20 Percent predicted a continuation of this rate of profits growth when CEO at the turn of the decade. This perfectly innocent piece of hubris acted as the kiss of death for the share price, and seemed to inadvertently change the business model from rat catching to profits warning issuance.

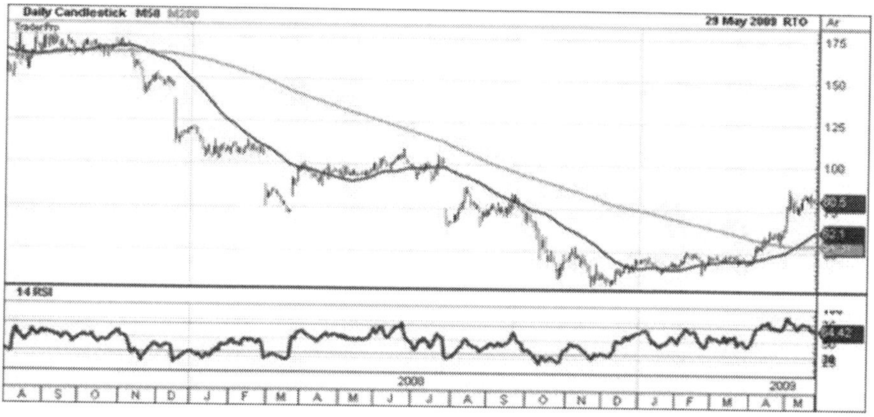

Clearly having already swallowed three profits warnings in the recent past, there would have been few in the market who did not have a cautious attitude to Rentokil's fundamentals. The technicals were, if anything, rather more straightforward than most such bear situations. This is because in addition to the classic 50/200 day moving average dead cross in November 2007 giving you an entry in the 140ps on the sell side, there was also a surprisingly simple sell signal from the gap below the post 2006 140p-180p range. This would have guided traders down to the island bottom buy signal in March 2008 from which an 86p entry on March 20th lead bottom fishers back to 100p in quick time.

But this is the point at which things started to become complicated.

While those looking at the stock on an extended time frame would have regarded Rentokil as remaining a short until there was a break back above the gap higher on July 17th gave a buy signal which was still open at the time of the 25th July warning. Flash/canny traders could have gone short at 104p on July 21st as the June 25th gap down was filled. According to this signal the stock would have been a short unless there was no end of day close above the gap, and there certainly was not. Nevertheless, it would appear that the market was genuinely relying on there being no more than three warnings. The end of the bear run finally came in the form of an October/November 2008 bear trap rebound combined with RSI bullish divergence, enough to triple the share price in less than a year.

61. Robert Wiseman Dairies (RWD): The Sharpest Profits Warning In The West September 16th 2010

It was not easy in a technical analysis book to make a reference to the late, politically incorrect (sexist) comedy giant Benny Hill via his number one hit single of 1971, but somehow this has been achieved. From a fundamental perspective one could say that the profits warning from the Scottish dairy group which supplies nearly a third of the UK's milk needs was a bolt from the blue. Helping to throw the bulls off the scent were comments earlier in the year that 2009-2010 had been a very satisfactory year, and in July that Q1 sales were up over 10%. Therefore September's warning of a H2 decline in profits of £7m was not the real hit here, it was the shock of caution after relative sweetness and light.

Competitive pressures were blamed, for the big turnaround which presumably meant that the group was suffering a supermarkets induced squeeze on margins.

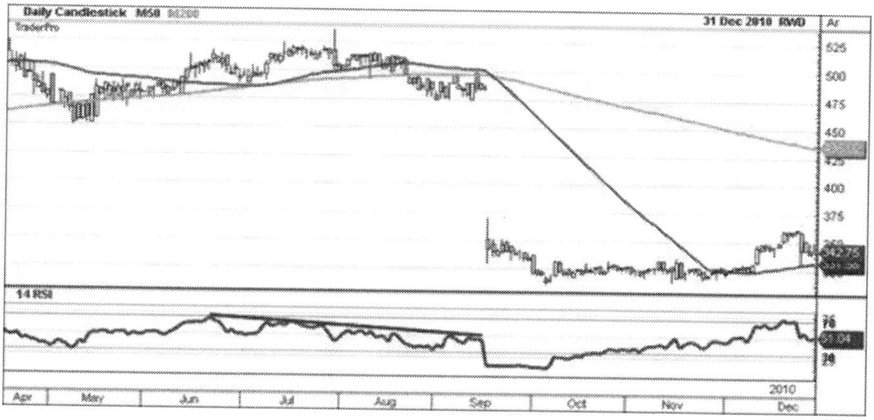

In contrast, the technical build up here was literally short and sweet. While the summer rolling top pattern above 500p was a matter of opinion, the end of day close below the 200 day moving average on August 20th at 490p was not as it could have been scanned for. The rule of three clear failures below the 200 day moving average and then down was completed on September 13th. Going into the profits warning day you may have been flat, you might have been lucky enough to be short, but being long was certainly difficult.

Another point that Robert Wiseman illustrates as far as all profits warnings is the strategy to adopt after the warning has been made. The day of the announcement in this case provided a 330p-370p range. This 370p is now the bottom of a vast gap and while below it on an end of day close basis one can regard the stock as an ongoing short. This could be especially true in this case due to the surprise effect of the reported fundamental turnaround. The days immediately after the news offered a chance to go short in the 340p's for those willing to risk up to 30p, and it was perhaps unfortunate for the bears that the decline subsequently was no lower than 310p.

62. ICAP (IAP): Follow The Leader February 5th 2010

There were only going to be three profits warnings examples. However, no selection could be complete without the run up to the February 5th 2010 profits warning from interdealer broker ICAP. While other examples are of theoretical shorts which could have been made, we have an actual deal that was carried out before the warning on January 11th at 440p. Given that there has been no subsequent report of wrongdoing by CEO and founder and Tory Treasurer Michael Spencer one has to assume that the sale of 8% of his holding in the company for £45m was skill, the kind of skill that makes you a billionaire.

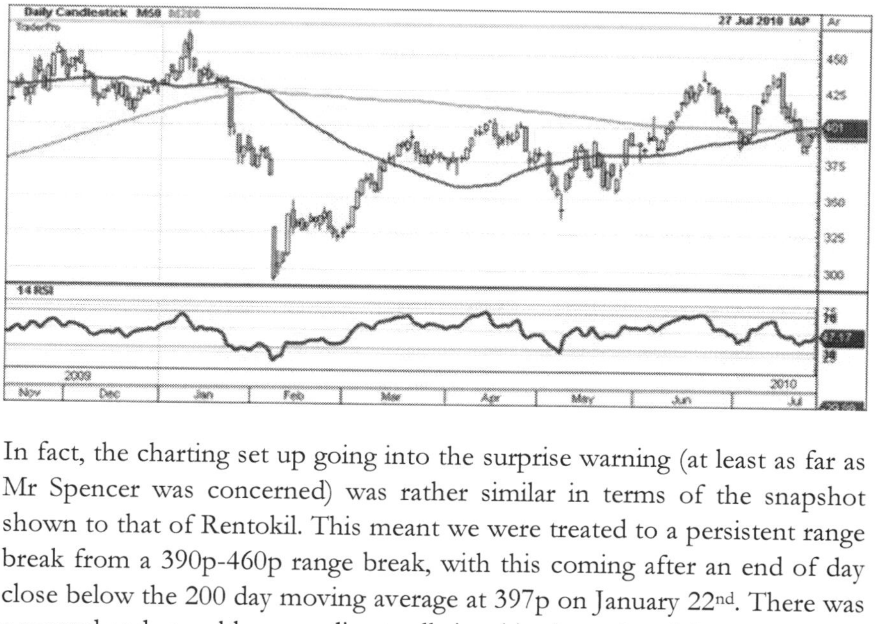

In fact, the charting set up going into the surprise warning (at least as far as Mr Spencer was concerned) was rather similar in terms of the snapshot shown to that of Rentokil. This meant we were treated to a persistent range break from a 390p-460p range break, with this coming after an end of day close below the 200 day moving average at 397p on January 22nd. There was a second and arguably more direct sell signal in the wake of the January 26th gap down that offered a 380p close level to sell at with an end of day close stop loss above the gap at 392p. This left traders comfortably in place for the early February warning. But it has to be admitted that even according to the methods we are following here the 440p exit price by our rich friend Mr Spencer is hard to beat.

A point to note here, and one probably explained by the way the shares had already fallen so far, is that the day of the profits warning turned out to be the low of the move. This is a very rare occurrence. In the case of ICAP one would have to say that the explanation is wholly due to the share sale, especially as the profits warning seems to have caught even the CEO on the hop.

BID RUMOURS: THE CHINESE WHISPERS GAME

In an ideal world the FSA would see that justice is done in the stock market – it would compensate victims of false/bogus bid stories which is where the ordinary shareholder really comes unstuck via the financial media and other less scrupulous sources. However, in order to justify its existence the guardian of the UK financial markets has been forced to get high profile results in flashy cases involving City slicker types that everyone hates.

Interestingly, it is surprising that in 2010 the FSA only found evidence of suspicious trading in advance of **30.6%** of UK takeovers. From a chartist's perspective I would suggest that the true figure is closer to 80%. The usual pattern of long entries a month-six weeks before confirmation of a deal, and then two weeks to go shakeout of the bulls is also a pattern I would like explained.

By definition there are far more bid rumours than actual M&A deals, and they materialise on an almost daily basis. Therefore knowing how to act when takeover rumours surface can be key. Mostly, by the time a stock is rumoured to be in play we are looking at the end of the line of a rally, but the charting picture will normally enable a technical trader to decide whether to buy, sell or hold if they are lucky enough to have already identified the shares as a prospect. Those confident of their charting abilities and not wishing to trade on a day to day basis could limit themselves to only companies said to be takeover candidates.

63. Rio Tinto (RIO): Billiton To Bid? 12th May 2007

It feels as if mining giant Rio Tinto is a perennial candidate for a takeover, and I suppose sometime in the next few years this will eventually happen, but there have been few years when serious bid speculation has not surrounded this company. In the recent past there have been two main contenders as far as taking Rio's independence, BHP Billiton (BLT) and the commodities hungry Chinese. In fact, given how we live in a world full of pen pushing/mouse clicking/business preventing over regulators, perceived competition issues mean that it would be very difficult for Billiton to ever achieve more than a lame partnership in certain areas of its business with rival Rio. But before the credit crunch started at the end of the summer of 2007 such minor issues were right at the back of traders' minds.

The Set Up

What is stand out as far as this example is concerned, is the way that from a bullish perspective we have an almost perfect charting set up prior to the bid rumour announcement in the financial press, and in the days and weeks following it. Indeed, the default with this chart and the accompanying fundamental catalyst is that it would give an impression that trading M&A rumours is as easy as falling off a log. If only this were the case.

The 2,132p bear trap low for Rio on March 14th left a gap to fill at 2,213p. Rather helpfully for the bull argument the following day Rio closed at

2,242p, a gap fill buy signal. Essentially, this was a perfect gift entry on a rally that would take the shares up more than 50% in just a few months. What is more there were no setbacks, fake outs, re- tests or any other monkey business. It was an easy ride. For the record, only an end of day close back below the March 14th low would have been a sell signal and in fact the result could have been as tight as an end of day close back below the top of the gap at 2,213p.

In fact, with such an early entry point, as it turned out, the buy signals that followed assumed the role of continuation signals. March 21st witnessed a 50/200 day moving average golden cross, and therefore it was understandable that the following day the shares gapped up, as they did on April 3rd, 5th and 16th. Indeed, the cue to take profits from 2,242 was the April 19th gap down and island top at 2,527p. The gap top left at 2,571p became the new long entry point on the end of day close of 2,613p on May 3rd, very handy for the fresh wave of gaps higher going into the May 12th (Saturday) newspaper story.

Outcome

Given the way that the shares had already come up nearly 800p from the lows, this could have been a great example of buy the rumour/sell the news, a decent stock market rule. But the charting reality was that the two unfilled May gaps represented a stock in technical overdrive. The key to whether there would be any setback was Rio remaining above the floor of the second gap of May 8th at 2,820p. Even with an entry of 3,006p – the high on the Monday after the news broke – there was an intraday low of 2,845p at worst, with a peak of 3,286p on June 18th.

Payoff

Rio in Q2 2007 was a situation which was a great technical set up before the bid rumour broke and from it we can take away the initial gap fill buy signal of March 15th. The golden cross simply backed up the trade. But as far as the aftermath of the bid rumour is concerned, it is evident that it was so far into the rally a charting road kill could have been the result. The only thing that saved those buying after the bid rumour news was the double unfilled gap. Indeed, the bull momentum was so strong that only the loss of the 200 day moving average in mid-July really suggested it was time to head for the exit.

64. ARM Holdings (ARM): Apple To Bid? June 10th 2010

It has been difficult to avoid ARM so many times in *101 Charts*, and I decided it should not be omitted in the bid rumour section just because of appearances elsewhere. This is an incredible company. Sticking with the incredible theme the rumour in June 2010 was that Apple (AAPL) might bid for the UK tech star. This is even though ARM's CEO Warren East had effectively poured cold water on the iPhone/Mac maker's reason to pay a few billion pounds to buy the whole company, when just getting it to provide its chip design services is a considerably more cost effective proposition. But why should things be so mundane?

The Set Up

The happy scenario as far as ARM was concerned by the time of the bid news story in the financial media – as much as reaction to the spike in the share price – was that those trading the shares regularly would/should have found it difficult to be anything other than long. The technical set up was very similar to that of the start of the bid rumour build up in Rio Tinto in 2007, with an exhaustion gap down, followed swiftly by an end of day close above the top of the gap to deliver a buy signal. This took traders long on a 239.5p close of May 26th versus a top of gap level of 236p. There was a mid-move continuation gap signal through the mid-250p's on June 3rd, enough of an incentive to remain long prior to the blow out peak of 362p on June 10th.

Outcome

This was one of those situations where the stock climbed in an accelerating fashion, and in some ways the only way of killing this speculation was for the share price to fly so high that there was no justification for such a big move without a significant fundamental driver. With nothing from Apple or anyone else as far as any intention to bid for ARM, and most likely all of those interested parties long for days or longer, this was a buy the stock ahead of the rumour, and take profits once the rumour is on the newswires.

Payoff

What the pie in the sky Apple to bid for ARM rumour illustrated is the benefits of being involved in a "hot stock" in that all of a sudden favourable speculation can blow your way. This means for any given signal such as a gap fill buy, whereas normally the result might be a 5% gain, in this instance 10-20% or more is possible. While this can also work against you, if a robust charting strategy is in place the risks can be minimized.

65. Invensys (ISYS): Bid Rumours – Siemens/GE? September 10th 2010

The Set Up

After fellow engineer Tomkins (TOMK) was taken over traders understandably wanted this old bid chestnut to be in play as well. But while one and one making three is something they really wanted to happen, it has to be admitted that even at the time the idea of Siemens or GE bidding for Invensys did not quite add up. Nevertheless, the message with any piece of M&A newsflow is to check the chart, and in the case of Invensys there were a couple of positive points.

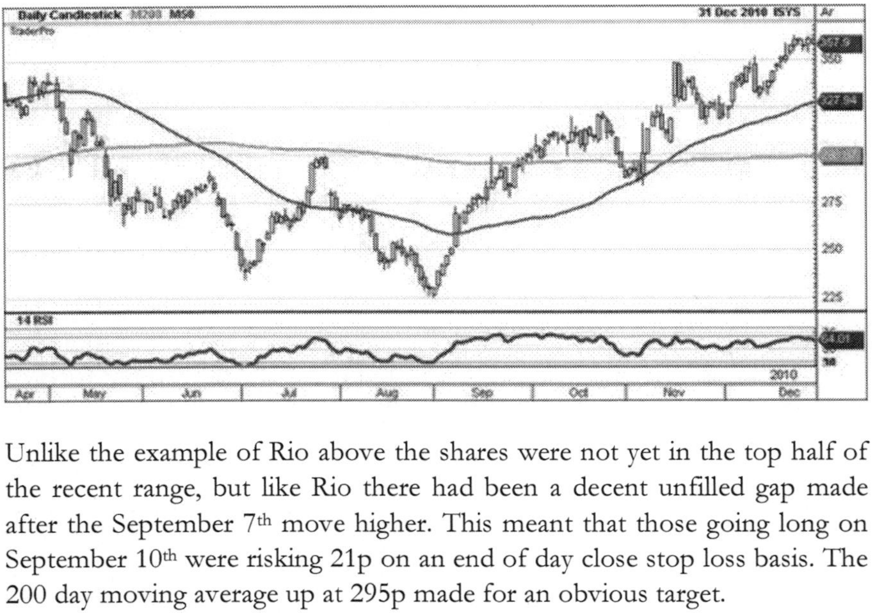

Unlike the example of Rio above the shares were not yet in the top half of the recent range, but like Rio there had been a decent unfilled gap made after the September 7th move higher. This meant that those going long on September 10th were risking 21p on an end of day close stop loss basis. The 200 day moving average up at 295p made for an obvious target.

Outcome

It was probably the case that the bid speculation associated with Invensys was tied in with relief that the shares had not been relegated from the FTSE 100, and this is something of a chicken and egg phenomenon as well. The bulls got a lucky break from the way that there was an end of day close back above the top of the July gap down at 292p on September 24th, which could have kept them in position beyond the initial target of the 200 day moving average. But essentially for longer term investors the unfilled gap down to 250p was the reason to remain in position, with or without the bid news.

Payoff

The coincidence of a lucky escape from FTSE 100 demotion, and the bid speculation and the way that the shares were relatively low in the trading range when the takeover rumour struck, meant that Invensys was an event worth noting in terms of the subsequent price action.

66. Home Retail Group (HOME): Walmart To Bid April 12th 2010

The Set Up

Whoever came up with the idea that US discount retailer Walmart (WMT) might be interested in bidding for the UK's Argos owner Home Retail Group must have had a cruel sense of humour. Indeed, this example is a good one for at least two reasons. The first is the way that the story was a particularly unrealistic one (it departed as quickly as it arrived), and it was also a challenge in terms of the technicals.

Outcome

One of the themes of this book is how special a gap through the 200 day moving average is. April 12th saw this happen to Home Retail, and accompanied by a bid story. The entry on the day was up to 295p, with an end of day close stop loss back below the gap, a set up that was to fail as the gap was filled. Indeed, the shares peaked out on April 26th at 300p and it was downhill all the way from that point.

While those going by the technical rulebook would have been sucked in close to the top and got away with losing say, 5%, April was a double top bull trap above the 200 day moving average, and both May and June witnessed unfilled gaps down. Great discipline was required not to stay in position on the off chance that the Walmart story had legs.

Payoff

The sad and often painful truth with bid rumours is that by the time they hit the financial headlines they are usually the top of the move on any rally, something which can be the case even if a deal actually materialises. As with real bid stories ideally, you are on board a situation on the basis of a gap fill, a bear trap or a moving average break, and it morphs into the start of a M&A story. As for the type of companies to be sniffing around as bid targets, I would venture that it is something which takes time to develop. The appropriate company tend to have a rather sleepy fundamental aura to them, but alas this is not in the remit of *101 Charts*. 101 Bids would be more appropriate.

BID SITUATIONS

In many ways the north face of the Eiger as far as a charting is concerned is the run up to a takeover bid, with the greedy and the good all alert for such situations. Ironically, there are probably easier and richer pickings in trying to identify profits warning, and almost no chance of getting sent to jail. But where is the fun in that?

Insider traders and more often failed insider traders scour the world over searching for such information, but the view of a technical trader is that all the inside information is in the price and can be legally gleaned. It will be seen on a significant proportion of occasions that charting setups can flag that it is time to be long of a stock. You may not know that any takeover is on its way, but may make a decent turn in any rally that precedes it, and sleep at nights. A review of some of the more outstanding takeovers of the recent past from a technical perspective should illustrate the typical twists and turns seen on charts prior to deals being announced. FSA take note, this could be useful.

67. BSkyB/News Corp: Cable TV

Out of a possible 60 million people in the UK eligible to be Business Secretary it is hard to imagine what the odds were on the democratic process of throwing up a Vince Cable. On the face of it would be an easier prospect to train a bull to run a china shop. But at least fans of News Corporation's offer for pay TV group BSkyB have had a lucky break in losing the prejudices of Mr Cable. The purpose of this exercise is however to see whether there were any charting cues as to a forthcoming deal.

The Set Up

Perhaps the first thing to consider with any bid announcement is what the chances of most traders/investors being long of the stock anyway actually were. In the case of BSkyB the fact is that the 200 day moving average had been rising as part of an uptrend nearly a year ahead of the June 2010 offer by News Corp to take full control of the group. So on this basis there was little problem. But it is the close detail on the daily chart as far as the days immediately before the June 15th gap up which are most intriguing.

Indeed, April/May witnessed a 10% plus setback for the shares back towards and below the 200 day moving average then at 562p. There then followed a magnificent buy signal in the form of an island bottom (gap down and then gap up). The implication of this is that a takeover approach on May 27th would have been perfect. Instead, June 3rd and June 4th actually combined to deliver an opposing sell signal in the form of an island top. While this was cancelled out by an end of day close above 573p on June

10th, only diehard chartists are likely to have been determined enough to keep chasing this situation.

Outcome

As we shall see with other bid situations that follow, as far as the run up to BSkyB was concerned, it was as if the price action going into June was ensuring that as few traders as possible would have been facing the right way by accident. True, the filling of the island top gap and the persistent support for the stock at and just below the 200 day moving average meant that we were biased to the long side, but there was no easy victory here. In fact, it is ironic that one would probably have been looking to buy the shares on the open of the day the deal was announced after a close above the inverted head and shoulders formation neckline/50 day moving average on June 14th.

Charting techniques would have brought short-term traders attention to BSkyB, but it is not clear whether many of them would have been able to get on board in this instance. The best way of illustrating this is to reveal the way that the model Portfolio of leading stocks on Zaks-TA.com was long of BSkyB going into the 100p plus surge, but on the basis that both the stock market and the shares were in a buy trend. That said the end of day close above the gap down on June 10th was a clear signal.

Payoff

Apart from the current and hopefully very soon former Business Secretary Vince Cable making a monkey out of himself regarding his rather biased views on the would be bidder of BSkyB, this situation provides us with a relatively typical blue chip M&A lead in as far as the charting position is concerned. The main point to note is the way that we actually have the best insight into a deal being on its way – or at least the bullish share price implications a month to three months prior to it happening.

Takeover speculation and reality in blue chip/FTSE 100 stocks is always going to be a difficult concept to conquer. You are up against the biggest brains, the strongest nerves and if you have a cynical view, the insider/informed traders who leave no trace of evidence and even if they did would never be brought to justice. But BSkyB was a gettable situation, even with the typical eve of deal (last week or two) pullback to shake off any casual longs. It is certainly worth remembering that for whatever reason the charting/trading picture is normally clearer two-three months ahead of time, rather than in the days immediately beforehand. Essentially, you have to go in early and then almost behave as if you will remain in position whatever you read in the financial media or whatever wobbles the share price makes.

68. Cadbury: Chocs Away

Cadbury bid speculation is something which was essentially where I came into the stock market on a day to day basis. The idea in 1989, at least according to the financial media, is that a takeover for the UK confectionary company was imminent, and would probably be a US group like say, Kraft Foods. This was bang on the money, apart from the minor detail that this speculation was 20 years early.

There are a couple of points that arise from the Cadbury story. The first is the way that there is of course no compensation system for people who buy a stock on a takeover rumour and lose money, and that it is not an offense to insider trade and lose money. You only incur the wrath of the law if you make money from a tip off from someone in the know. As I chartist I am arrogant enough to think that money can be made just by looking at the charts (on the basis that the trail of those who are hot on the trail of a deal will be evident in the price pattern/volume. I am also not that motivated by money . . . But the reality I see is that the only losers from insider trading in bid situations are those who are caught short of the stock (evil people anyway) and spreadbetting companies from whom their profits are being taken.

Indeed, my guess is that the spreadbetters are the whistleblowers to the FSA. It cannot be difficult for these companies to spot the "guilty" parties given that 90% of their short term traders lose money. The individual with a sudden six figure overnight balance in his account cannot be difficult to spot, especially when the spreadbet company has to find this money out of its own pocket. Nevertheless, this person has in buying stock before a deal is announced helped to propel its share price higher than it would have gone if he had not bought. This is not something that most shareholders would really complain about, or regard as criminal injustice.

In contrast, if there is an enemy to the ordinary shareholder it is those bears who short (with insider knowledge) prior to a profits warning or other disastrous news, something which was seen in the likes of Northern Rock, HBOS and other leading UK banks in 2008. Even here though, and in the wake of the idiotic (and unfair) shorting ban soon after, it is actually very difficult to pinpoint a situation when unfair damage was meted on a company by such speculation.

If a bear is wrong he will lose money in a sudden and swift fashion. For some reason the financial media never mentioned the way that bears get burned when they are wrong, only that they make money when they are right. The wisest thing that Margaret Thatcher said is that you cannot buck the market. What she could have added is that this means you should never try and tinker with it either as your actions can blow up in your face – the concept of the shorting ban comes to mind.

The Set Up

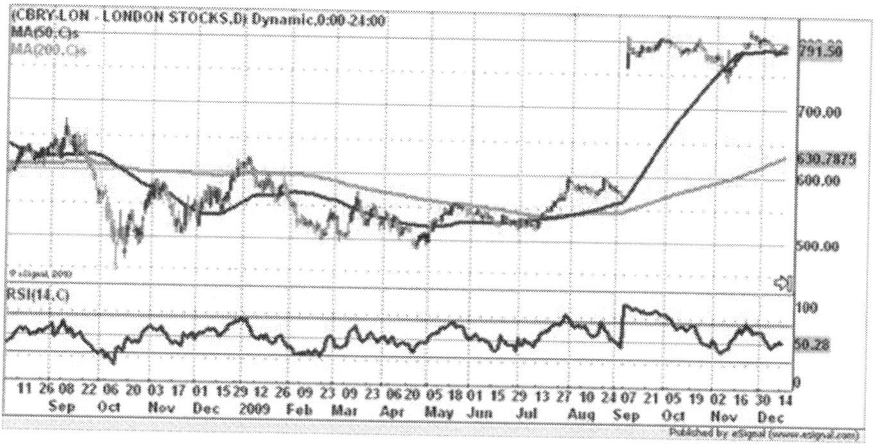

Having had 20 years to be prepared for a possible Cadbury takeover, it is perhaps not surprising that I was on the case in early 2009 as over the previous two decades. Helping out was the way that by the end of April we had been treated to four main tests of support at and just below the 500p level. The start of the real action – ironically, quite often the case – came via a gap to the downside on April 22nd. Indeed, the early bird buy signal was the end of day close above the gap at 510p on May 5th. This echoed what was seen at the start of the BSkyB bid approach the following year and underlines how important gaps are to charting. For Cadbury the share price never fell below 510p again.

Phase two of the build-up to the bid in Cadbury came not surprisingly with another gap, this time to the upside and in close proximity to the 200 day moving average. Indeed, such gaps just below, above and especially through the 200 day moving average are among the strongest buy signals at any time for stocks/markets. In this example it was actually a gap through the 50 day moving average and end of day close above the 200 day line which at the time provided an entry point on the buy side at let us say 544p on July 15th, with only an end of day close below the bottom of the gap at 523p the stop loss. In fact, this never came close to happening and Cadbury shares moved up nearly 10% by the end of the month.

The start of August delivered a golden cross between the 50/200 day moving averages with the message being that you would only consider taking a profit here on an end of day close below the 50 day line at the earliest, and preferably only on a failure below the 200 day moving average. As of the start of 2011 we have similar buy and hold set ups for the FTSE 100 and Gold.

Outcome

As far as the set up for Cadbury (if you ignore the 20 year lead in time) I would give this no more than a 7 or 8 out of 10, even though the bull run was flagged by extended 500p support, a golden cross and a pair of gaps. This is because in the month or so before the confirmation of a rejected bid approach from Kraft on September 7th 2009 when the stock gapped up over 200p to 783p there had been a rather obvious double top at 600p. The impression is that much of the near term money had actually given up on a deal, an idea backed up by the bearish divergence in the RSI window between the two 600p zone highs. And of course, how could it be any other way?

A takeover in a FTSE 100 company is not something which can be easily disguised for a number of obvious reasons (everyone is watching), especially if you go along with the idea that a key purpose of the financial markets is to move in the direction of the greatest loss for the greatest number of participants. All the bullish signals were in place well ahead of time, but that final pullback before the announcement would have shaken out a large proportion of those who had correctly guessed that after years Cadbury was about to lose its independence.

Payoff

The message as far as getting on the back of the big blue chip bid is not to clutch defeat from the jaws of victory. Even the most certain deals will have days before they are confirmed when it appears either from the price action or the newsflow that the game could be up. However, this is a game where standing firm and sticking to big picture money management levels will pay off, with gaps and rising near term moving averages particularly important. To use an everyday cliché, the darkest hour (when you feel like closing out your buy position) could very well be before the dawn (the day the bid is confirmed.)

69. Dana Petroleum (DNX): A High Octane Takeover

It probably says as much about my prejudices regarding the oil & gas explorers that I managed to largely ignore the build-up to Dana Petroleum's takeover, something which was not only a shame because this avoidance was based on a perception that did not have any logical backing. Instead, it was a view that the situation would be too hairy to make a call on. Having not studied the charting build up here I will find out whether I was right to avoid this situation or not, a process which should be useful to anyone who talks about "the one that got away" in relation to the stock market in particular or financial markets as a whole. For instance, I would be quite certain that there are many who avoided Gold/Gold stocks because they are "too high" or say, utility stocks because they are "too boring" even if one of them happened to be International Power (IPR.) The list could go on and on.

The Set Up

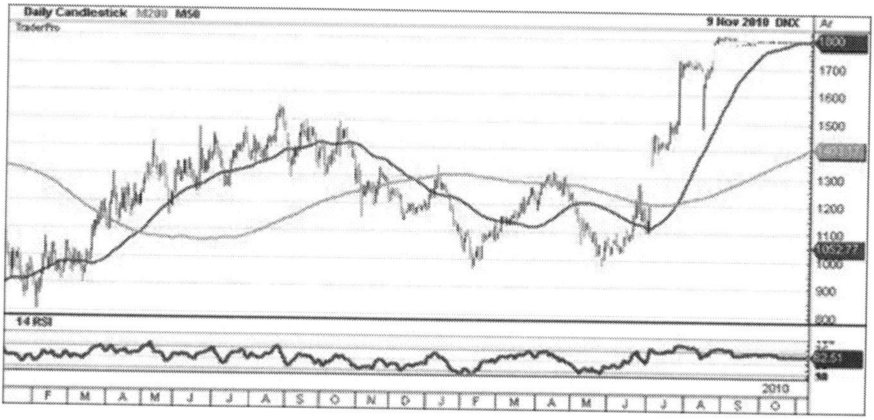

It is somewhat surprising that going into the early July 2010 jump for Dana, the shares appeared to be trading in a rather pressured range up to the 1,300p zone/200 day moving average. Indeed, January, April and June delivered three major 200 day line failures, something which explains why a casual observer of the stock might not regard it as being that appealing. Nevertheless, there are several reasons for those who stayed on the sidelines to kick themselves.

The story starts in February with an island bottom between the 4th and 15th, something which guided the shares via the 20 day moving average to a 1,250p plus destination over the following month. Just in case you missed out on this there was a double island bottom formation between May 25th and June 10th. Within 2 weeks the shares had peaked out above the 200 day moving average for a 1,250p plus destination versus an entry point at 1,100p or better. The cue to take profits was the late June failure at and below the 200 day line then around 1,210p, just days before the July 2nd bid approach announcement.

Outcome

The bad news with Dana is that the share price succumbed to the "typical" two week to go pre-bid pullback – a mysterious but unfortunately rather consistent phenomenon. The good news is that the gap higher for the shares off the back of KNOC bid approach news delivered a gap through the 200 day moving average. Clearly on this occasion the stop loss would not be an end of day close back below the gap at 1,200p, but the top of the gap at 1,340p – still approaching a 100p risk – was a possible trade for aggressive traders given the announcement that Dana was in play. In the end the risk of 100p compared quite reasonably with the 250p upside eventually delivered up to the end of July. And the story did not end there. The late July 50/200 day moving average golden cross meant that we were biased to the long side from then on, so that the August 12th gap down sell signal could have been ignored – it seems wise to ignore sell signals while in the aftermath of a golden cross between the 50/200 lines. An end of day close above the 1,687p on August 17th delivered another 100p plus upside, and effectively closed the best of the charting based speculation associated with the Dana takeover.

Payoff

There was some compensation here for the way that immediately prior to the July 2nd bid approach announcement there was a good chance that most traders were either flat or had taken profits. The gap higher of that day held and there was a swift and satisfying push to the upside. I am yet to work out how and why share prices of the bid situations covered in *101 Charts* have the pre-confirmation dip, maybe a friendly market maker can help solve the mystery?

70. Wellstream (WSM): Going With The Flow

Although M&A speculation on oil & gas explorers is something which cautious traders might be excused for avoiding, if only on the basis that even the best of them can deliver painful share price setbacks in the wake of drilling failures, an oil services sector stock such as Wellstream can appear to be a more reliable prospect. In fact, during 2008 these shares fell from over 1,400p to under 300p. Fast forwarding to 2010 and the shares were still base building in an erratic fashion.

The Set Up

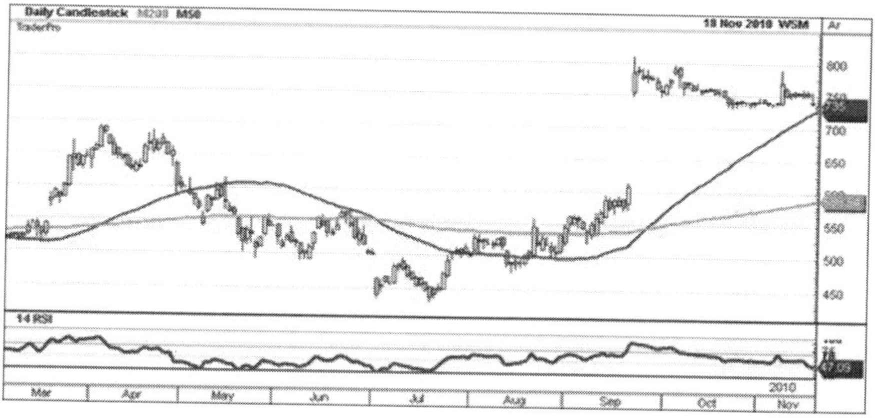

While Wellstream may not be a big company in terms of market capitalisation, it eventually accepted an £800m bid from General Electric in December 2010, the sequence of technical/charting signals is typical of what one may expect in the run up to a bid. The main stand out here is that if anything, the lead into the deal was somewhat less fraught than usual.

The big plus here was actually the start of Wellstream being in focus as a possible buy off the back of July's combination of a bear trap double bottom in the price window and RSI bullish divergence on the second lower price low on July 19th at 420p. In fact, it could be argued that this bear trap was nasty enough to ensure that no subsequent flushing out of the bulls would be required. Instead, there was a RSI trendline that could be drawn which lasted unbroken (keeping the longs in position) until well after the September 22nd confirmation of multiple preliminary bid approaches.

Outcome

Those who were really on the ball had a buy opportunity off the back of bullish RSI divergence on the end of day close back above the July 435p intraday low on July 20th. The fill of the June 28th gap to the downside on August 2nd on a 527.5p close was the rather less flashy long entry as an end of day close above the 515p gap top. Following this were the now customary pre-takeover 200 day moving average failures and assorted flushing out attempts, but there was no cause to exit due to the support from the early warning RSI uptrend line from the beginning of July. This was particularly useful in early August where buyers had no reason to even blink on the bear trap below the 50 day moving average.

Nevertheless, while some traders would have been buying and clinging on to Wellstream, there was a final sweet buy signal coming in the form of a September 8th end of day close gap fill/200 day moving average rebound which delivered a 550p buy price. It was only two weeks after that the shares were standing at 750p. But once again, the September 7th gap down could and perhaps even should have unnerved "casual" longs.

Payoff

Wellstream was perhaps as good as it gets in terms of a stock providing a well flagged buy opportunity which was initially of the bottom fishing variety, but then progressed into an M&A situation which had no disappointments up its sleeve. What appealed most here was the mix of different signals from gap fills to divergence to the bear trap double bottom.

COMMODITIES CORNER: THE START OF THE SUPERCYCLE IN GOLD

71. Gold 1999-2002

Although it may appear that cover in commodities is not strictly on topic as far as a guide to stock market success is concerned, I would argue that one of the best ways of trading alterations in the likes of gold and oil is via exploration companies in the respective areas. For instance, the gearing effect can really kick in as far as the relationship between the underlying commodity and stocks in the sector. If Gold rallies from $1,000 an ounce to $1,400 an ounce, a rise of 40%, a basket of Gold stocks might double or triple over this period. Of course, a similar fall in Gold would see stocks in the relevant sector decline by a half or a third – so you need to get your timing right as the magical effect of operational gearing is a two edged sword.

The Set Up

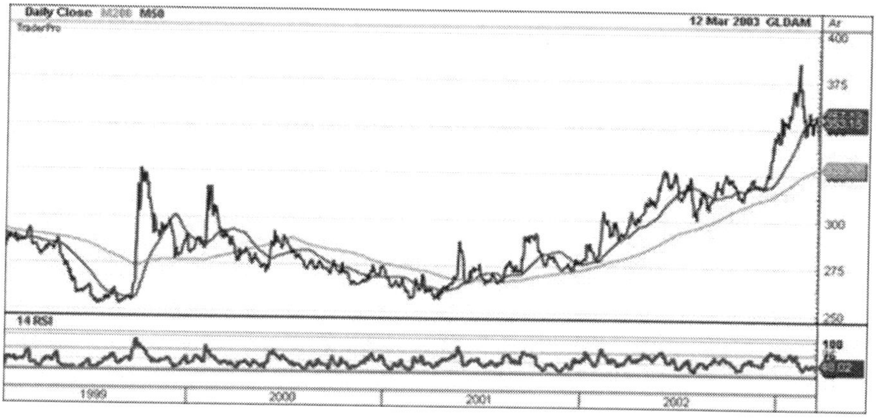

The charting seeds of the great bull run in Gold that we are currently experiencing were sown right at the end of the millennium in 1999. While it may be wrong to suggest that this was an easy situation to get in on at the ground floor, it was not obvious enough to the then Chancellor of the Exchequer Gordon Brown to prevent him selling the bulk of the UK's gold reserves over the next three years. What we see on a daily chart of the metal are lower price lows was the metal starting in June 1999 contrasting sharply with higher highs in the RSI window – an extended bullish divergence oscillator buy signal.

This would normally be a reason to get involved, if only on a short-term basis. However, the break above the 50 day moving average and subsequently the 200 day moving average then at $274 suggested that we should maintain a keen interest in this market. This is over and above the fact that there was a near vertical move for Gold in September and October. While there was still some months and consolidation either side of the time of the 200 day moving average to endure, the technical splash of early autumn 1999 really did smack of the smart money getting into position.

Outcome

It is a sad fact of the financial markets that most government intervention to support or defend levels delays psychological or otherwise, or work betting against. George Soros illustrated this in shorting Sterling on a massive basis as the UK attempted to remain in the ERM in 1992, and Japan attempting to weaken the yen in order to defend the cause of its exporters remains an ongoing cue to buy the Japanese currency on dips. But the big prize goes to Gordon Brown in providing such a brilliant, unwitting buy signal, albeit one that was based on the hubris of the time that inflation was dead along with the boom/bust cycles of the economy.

72. The Dawn of the Gold Supercycle: Rio Tinto

The Set Up

As will be seen with the example of Cairn Energy below, the setup of Rio Tinto ahead its underlying commodity turnaround was very similar to that of the oil explorer – especially the antics relative to the falling 200 day moving average. This of course backs the idea of investigating stock price action at such times. As far as Rio is concerned the highlight of the daily chart over this period is the inverted head & shoulders. While even at the best of times such reversals patterns can be difficult to spot, the start of the formation in May 1998 was announced by a gap down below the red neckline, and then a gap up above the same neckline in February 1999. Aggressive traders had the chance of an entry point on the December RSI rebound bear trap down to 536p, but the conventional entry point was the February gap, with only an end of day close below the neckline at 620p (just below the floor of the gap at 622p).

Outcome

The implied upside target was based on the 180p depth of the inverted head & shoulders formation (August 1998 low to October 1998 high) and perhaps not surprisingly this was easily exceeded. There was an almost straight run to the upside up to April 1999 with a celebratory gap that month on the way. The peak after that was 1,200p plus reached on the first session of 2000.

Payoff

For the greater part of my charting career I was a slave to identifying million dollar charting patterns such as head & shoulders, rectangle breaks and the like. My emphasis now is to only use them if they force me to do so. This was certainly the case as far as Rio in 1998/9 with the gaps starting and finishing the bull run. If only there was normally such clarity.

73. The Dawn of the Gold Supercycle: BHP Billiton (BLT)

The Set Up

The set up for BHP in 1998/1999 is one that rather leaves me wondering where to begin. This is because it could have been approached from so many angles. Perhaps the easiest is the red 1998 trendline/50 day moving average break of February 8th 1999 for a 126p notional entry. Otherwise the end of day close above the top of a February 16th gap down at 135p on the 26th of the month, or even any weakness towards the multi tested 200 day moving average then at 129p during March, or under 150p towards the end of the month in the wake of a golden cross between the 50/200 day moving averages. The bulls were really spoilt for choice, especially as aggressive traders could have been buying the stock on any dips towards the post June RSI support line from November to January – in a range between 130p down to 110p.

Outcome

Billiton delivered it all in 1999, with the break of an extended falling trendline, the falling 50 day moving average, a rebound off an extended RSI uptrend line over six months old and repeated tests for support after the break above the 200 day moving average. After such a show it was not exactly surprising that the shares were not far from doubling in a matter of weeks. Also worth watching out for is the way that after the initial break above neutral RSI 50 in February, the oscillator managed to remain above neutral 50 until well into May – quite a testimony to the strength of the turnaround.

Payoff

BHP Billiton's turnaround in early 1999 reminds us of the way that (magically) mining stocks have a happy knack of moving ahead of metals prices and while the reverse may be true on the way down, this may not be too much of a worry for those who in 2010 expect Gold and other precious metals to be 50% or more higher than where they are currently over the next couple of years.

THE PEAK OIL SPIKE

74. Crude Oil

As we shall see with a couple of examples in terms of oil explorers and stocks, the period immediately before the start of the Credit Crunch crisis of 2008 saw a fantastic countermove bubble in many leading assets. Perhaps the most dramatic was the one seen in Crude Oil (WTI) in 2007-2008. What was particularly interesting here is the way that the overshoot to the upside continued even as the rug was being pulled from under the banking sector. Indeed, we can focus on both the start of the rally and the technicals that brought it down on a chart that covers a relatively small period.

The Set Up

While ongoing geopolitical issues such as those seen in the Middle East, North Korea and Iran are the conventional explanation for the rise in crude oil over the mid-2000s period, along with the ravages of Hurricane Katrina in 2005, it is now clear that none of these factors taken individually or as a whole were enough to explain how crude oil doubled over such a short period of time. Instead, it makes more sense that the booming global economy and fears over Peak Oil were really the best explanation of the spike. In fact, along with the Peak Oil hysteria conspiracy theorists may wish to add the notion that why this period hedge fund and other renegade speculators were perfectly capable of kicking this market around like a football. Similar feeding frenzies have since been seen in agricultural commodities and rare earth metals.

Outcome

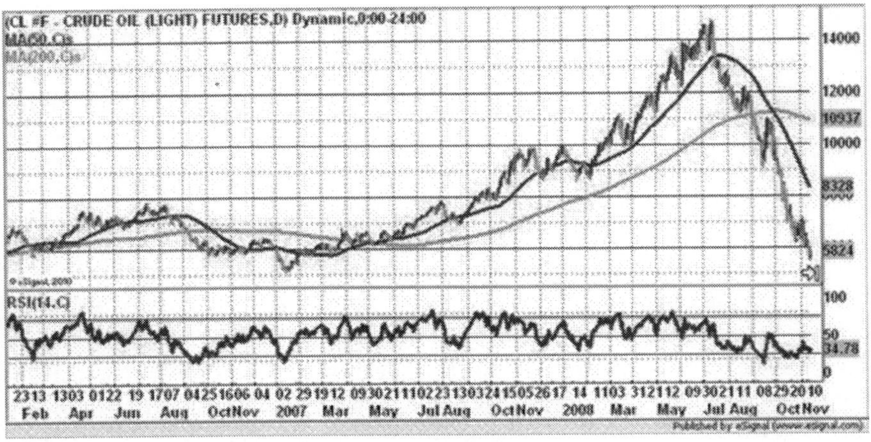

The start of the Peak oil rally at the end of 2006 came in the form of a January countermove low towards $50 which would have had the effect to stop loss out the bulls who had spotted the party was about to begin just a little too early. But those big buy signals came from the way that there was significant bullish divergence in the RSI window between the price lows of autumn 2006 and the initial 2007 support.

In fact, I would suggest that the really golden opportunity to go long of this market came in the wake of the March, April, May triple test of support at and just below the 200 day moving average then at $62. This is a formidable bull signal on any stock or market, and certainly proved its mettle as far as delivering a doubled price for this market. In contrast, the end of the line came from bearish divergence in the RSI window from June 2008 where a higher highs above $130 left the oscillator stranded below the overbought 70 mark. Something to remember off the back of the peak in the Peak Oil is the way that related stocks will sink before the underlying commodity, just as in the way that they will tend to front run the start of a sustained move higher.

75. Peak Oil Stocks: Cairn Energy (CNE)

The Set Up

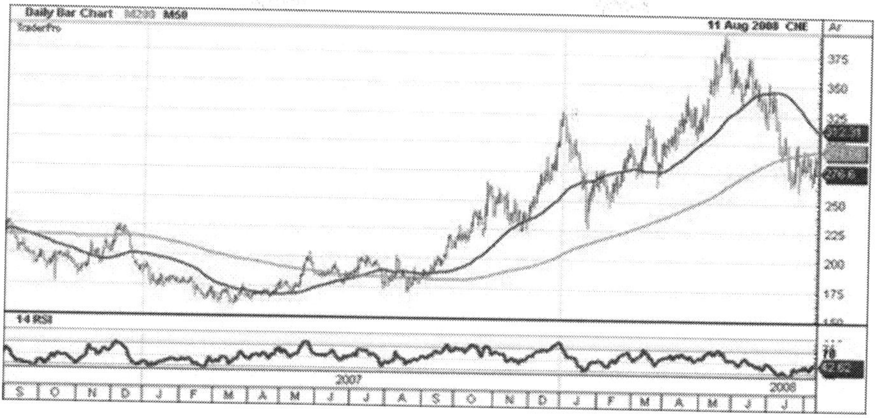

Cairn Energy provided a decent mirror to the activities of the underlying commodity, even though the low for the stock came around two months after the low in Crude Oil. This is because it can be seen from the daily chart/RSI trace that the stock was essentially bumping along the bottom from late 2006. The first possible entry point for Cairn was in mid-March with the bear trap towards 150p and the higher RSI low above the 2007 support line. However, the safest and least obscure buy point here was the late August combination of a third bounce off the January 2007 support line accompanied by a break above the 200 day moving average. A gap through the 50 day moving average on September 7th around 180p and then another gap on September 19th meant there was another entry point in the low 190p's with little reason to change the bullish stance until the 50 day moving average was lost around 250p in January 2008.

Outcome

It was somewhat surprising that there was such a long set up period for Cairn in 2007. This is said despite the very positive cup & handle pattern and despite the way that oil & gas explorers rarely need more than a whiff of a possible find, or rising underlying commodities prices to get going on the upside.

In this case a substantial rally was preceded by an extended slide either side of the 200 day moving average between May and September 2007, something which would almost certainly have frustrated or shaken out all but the most ardent of bulls/those who were looking for a crude oil proxy play. Adding to the degree of difficulty were three lower lows in June, July and August.

Payoff

If you had picked out Cairn as your Peak Oil play you would have had to consider yourself unlucky in terms of picking out a stock so determined to shake out the longs. It would be great to suggest a way of avoiding such problematic positions, but alas this is all part of the rich fabric of the resources area in particular and the financial markets as a whole.

76. Peak Oil Stocks: Tullow Oil (TLW)

The Set Up

It could be said that there was more risk and more reward on tap for those who had decided to go for Tullow Oil as their big oil & gas sector play for 2007 than at Cairn Energy. At the same time the set up chartwise was that much more straightforward. We were treated to both a quadruple bottom for the shares between January and May as well as a RSI support line. To add to the availability of this buy prospect was the proximity of the 200 day moving average in the 385p zone for much of H1 2007 – with any sustained break of this feature suggesting a fresh leg to the upside.

Outcome

The action for bulls of Tullow Oil was delivered in staggered, and unusually discreet ways. The first buy signal was likely to have been missed by most as it was an end of day close above the top of a May 4th chart gap at 369p. This occurred on May 17th and suggested that one would go long on the basis of the closing price of that day at 376p. An end of day close below the 50 day moving average was the initial dynamic stop loss. A gap up on May 14th followed by an end of day close at 395p above the 200 day moving average delivered a new buy signal with the stop loss an end of day close back below the narrow gap at 382.75p. From this point the shares really took off with no less than three gaps up to 500p. The usual rule is that anything more than two unfilled gaps either to the upside or downside and you should remain in position in expectation of substantial gains.

In fact, the Tullow Oil charting adventure did not finish with the bearish RSI divergence top in July. The shares were cheeky enough to fill the June gaps up during August down to the 200 day moving average. The intraday rebound from this feature was backed by a gap through the 50 day line on a 483p close buy to propel the stock towards 700p by November. Even using the overly generous 50 day moving average as an end of day close stop loss the second gap buy signal was worth over 100p.

Payoff

If nothing else the 2007 price action of Tullow Oil illustrates what an adventure charting resources stocks can be, as well as suggesting that getting involved in this area may not be the casino many believe it to be. Of course, it helps to only get involved with clear charting signals in the way of gaps, moving average breaks and RSI cues, but if complex price action is broken down in a rational way the rewards can be significant.

LONG-DISTANCE STOCK CHARTING: STRETCHING THE TIMEFRAMES

One of the realities of the markets in recent years is that with the internet and margined trading, as well as the greater prevalence of technical analysis, timeframes for trading have shrunk to hours or days rather than weeks or months. The old saying was that a long term investment is a short term one that went wrong. Over the past decade in all too many examples this has been the case. The nature of the price action even in the blue chip zone can mean that unless you have very deep pockets or a timeframe of more than a decade getting your money back can be a challenge. At least for the examples of BT (BT.A) and Vodafone (VOD) I shudder to think how long those who bought near the top will have to wait. But what will be seen from the charts is that the warning signs were in place beforehand.

77. Barclays (BARC): 2000-2010 Weekly Chart

Although the newly appointed CEO of Barclays Bob Diamond is someone I would be afraid to meet in a dark alley, or in fact any alley, the stock is included as a tribute to the good work Mr Diamond did for BarCap. This is in addition to the incredible coup in mopping up the best bits of the fallen/pushed Lehman Brothers, and the wonderful contribution to Anglo/Mid East relations in terms of the stakes and profits offered to Abu Dhabi and Qatar when Barclays understandably did not want to avail itself of a UK taxpayer bailout.

Rather surprisingly after all this, on a ten year view it can be seen how the bias is still on the downside for Barclays shares. While you might not feel like going short of the shares, the message as of the end of 2010 was that since the financial crisis hit in mid-2008 the stock has continued to fail at and below the former 2003 support of 310p. Indeed, only sustained price action above the lost 2000 support line/200 week moving average at 379p over the next year or two would really get Barclays back on the bull tack. While it currently seems almost ridiculous there is still an outside chance of a partial or even full retest of the 2009 support below 60p if we do not see the low 300p's zone recovered early in 2011.

78. BT Group (BT.A): 2000-2010 Weekly Chart

I remember the beginning of the end of the BT bull run that accompanied the dot-com Bubble, the rumour that Telefonica of Spain was about to bid. This propelled the share price through 1,400p for the last time in 2000, and it was all downhill from there. The loss of the ten week moving average at the beginning of April when the stock was still above 1,100p provided a decent early warning that something was amiss for the bulls, but it has to be admitted that as with most of the post dot-com bubble declines, the possibility of a 90% loss from the best levels was something that appeared close to ridiculous.

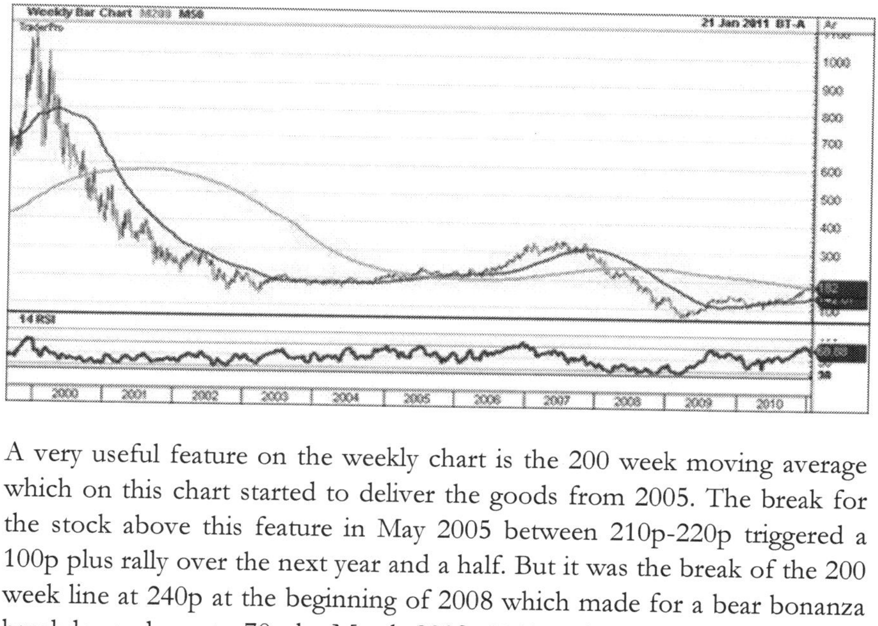

A very useful feature on the weekly chart is the 200 week moving average which on this chart started to deliver the goods from 2005. The break for the stock above this feature in May 2005 between 210p-220p triggered a 100p plus rally over the next year and a half. But it was the break of the 200 week line at 240p at the beginning of 2008 which made for a bear bonanza breakdown down to 70p by March 2009. 2010 ended with an initial failure at the still falling 200 week line, which will take quite some beating even if the bulls eventually prevail.

79. Prudential (PRU): 2000-2010 Weekly Chart

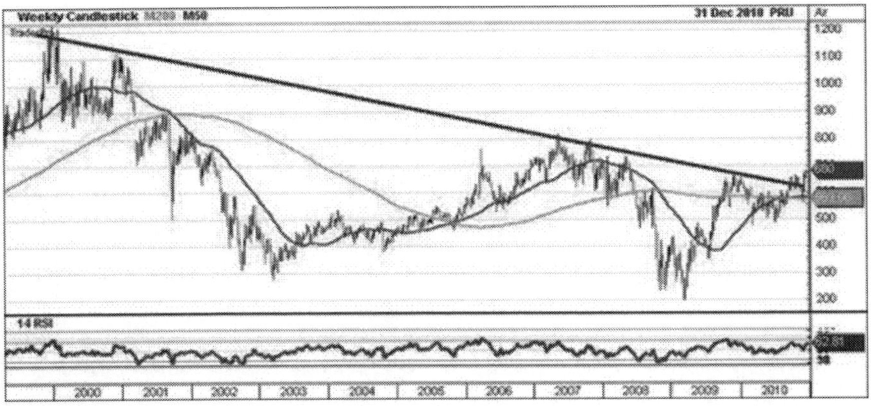

Prudential is about the hottest weekly chart among leading UK stocks at the end of our timeframe up to 2010. This is because going into the end of this year the shares managed to bounce off the 50 and 200 week moving averages just below 570p, and break the resistance line from the beginning of 200 nominally running through 640p. The rather exciting prospect going into 2011 is that we have a stock delivering a major trend change, and one that could hopefully last for years. The stop loss is the choice between a weekly close back below 640p – the broken decade long trendline, and the 200 week moving average at 569p for those with deep pockets.

If nothing else, this is a just reward for shareholders of the insurer after a year in which they were staring down the barrel of uncertainty as the possibility of a multibillion Pound deal valued at nearly twice the market capitalisation of the Pru could have been in play. Luckily, institutional shareholders managed to prevent the danger of RBS/ABN mark II, and after a series of wobbles we have seen the downtrend in the stock snapped, at least for now.

80. Vodafone (VOD): 2000-2010 Weekly Chart

The weekly chart of mobile phone operator Vodafone reminds us how the telecoms segment was caught up in the mania of 1999-2000 and how the period of reckoning continues in a painful fashion as far as long term shareholders are concerned. Indeed, it could be argued that at least for some stocks and sectors the rather dramatic tag of the "death of equities" is actually not too wide of the mark.

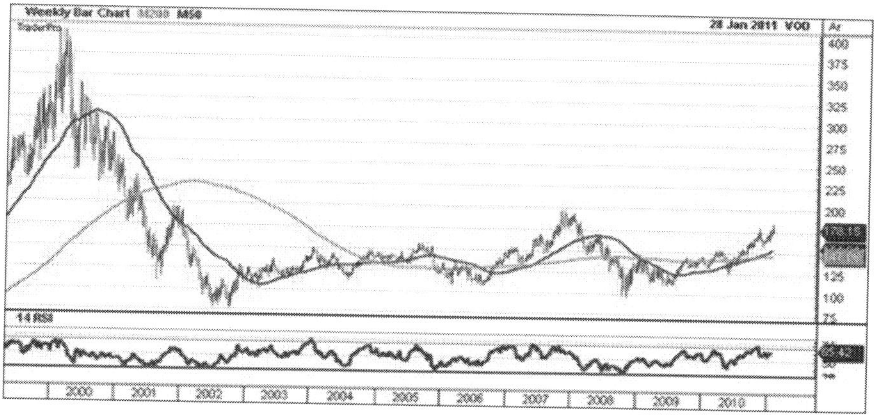

The problem we had to face at the end of 2010 is that a nine year plus period of consolidation, or perhaps more accurately regrouping, had been taking place. Within this extended problem there are further issues. The worst is the way that for instance even the golden 50/200 week moving average golden crosses of 2006 and 2010 were followed by decent intermediate rallies, but could not kill the extended bear market here.

Indeed, it is hard to see what will apart from the obvious – a weekly close back above the 2007 peak of 197.5p. Unfortunately, there does not appear to be any sense in buying a chronic underperformer at the top of its range. More appealing would be the idea of buying the floor of a rising trend channel in place since the beginning of 2002 and based at the current position of the 200 week moving average at 146p. But it can be said that overall Vodafone is exactly the kind of charting situation where the best thing is to avoid doing anything at all unless it really demonstrates fresh and sustained new strength. If this does not sound like a recipe for stock market success, I would insist that it is. There is nothing so valuable as knowing when not to get involved.

PENNY STOCKS CORNER: JOLLY HOCKEY STICKS

For years, until the start of the commodities stocks boom in the late 2000s, I made a deliberate attempt to ignore the small caps and penny stocks arena, particularly the single figure penny stocks. It now seems to me that this omission could very well be the main reason I am neither a multimillionaire nor penniless – touch wood.

I fell for the idea that without liquidity and decent charting history it is not possible to predict price action. In fact, on many occasions this is not relevant and can even be an advantage. Therefore, if you hear that I have run off to buy an island in the Caribbean and am no longer advising others on how to invest/trade it is likely that I have done so via penny share punting. A couple examples follow of recent classic penny stock breakouts.

81. Niche Group (NGP): Finding Its Place

The hockey stick comment to head up this section is a snipe on the global warming fraud whereby a chart of rising temperatures over the past 1,000 years is virtually a flat horizontal line which then has the rise in the 20th century appear as the end of a hockey stick. While this has not prevented the coldest December for 100 years in the UK for 2010, one can apparently still look forward to bikini clad sunbathers every winter by the Serpentine by the of the 21st century. Well, we would except for the problem of London being below sea level by that time.

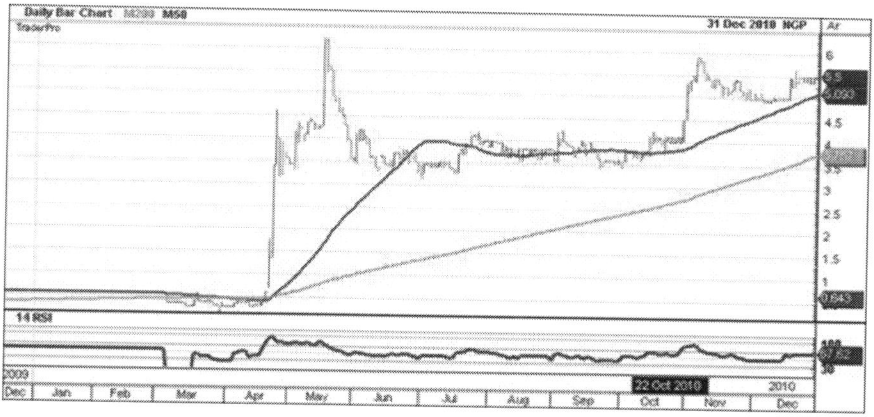

The daily chart of Niche Group is perhaps typical of what you would ideally like to see in terms of a single stock starting its ascent. The key here is to look firstly for support on daily ranges coming in at or above the 200 day moving average, and then the 200 day moving average itself starting to rise. The share price crossing and closing above the 200 day line can be scanned for using TraderPro from Updata, as can the latest stocks to witness a turn up in this longer term moving average.

As far as Niche was concerned July 20th 2009 was the fateful day when a stop gapped up above the 200 day moving average on an end of day close at 0.3p. Two sessions later the stock had peaked out just below 1.2 pence to deliver an astounding percentage gain. This was just the start. The price action lift meant that both the 200 day and 50 day moving averages were both rising to a golden cross from the end of July so that from that point on one could regard Niche as a super bullish situation. Any weakness towards the 200 day line could be regarded as a buying opportunity, although in these situations it is probably best just to go long first and quibble about the exact merits of different entry levels later. Even if you had paid a penny for the stock during 2009 by May the following year the shares were standing at 6 pence.

82. Beowulf Mining (BEM): Who's Afraid of the Bull Run?

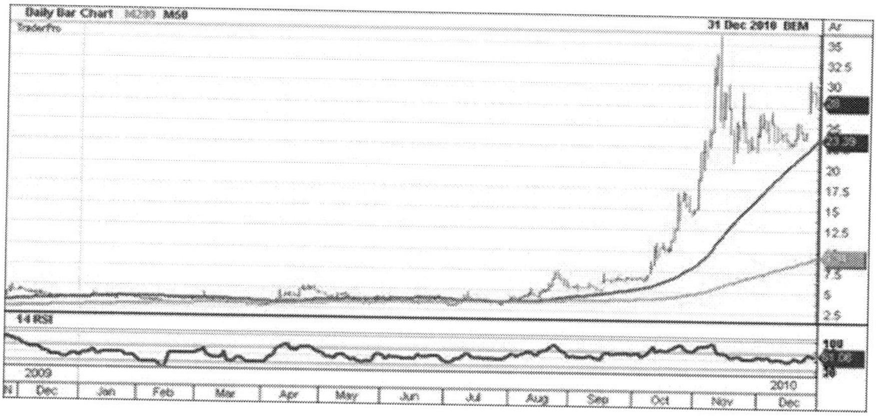

This is such a classic in terms of the bull run which gradually accelerates gaining more and more momentum on the daily chart. Helping out here was a spike up for this stock through the 200 day moving average in April 2010 then at 3p. By September the technicals were implying that while the September gap higher remained unfilled down to 5.3p we had flipped to severe bull mode.

Even those not prepared to put up with the rather rocky ride initially had already been treated to a 50/200 day moving average golden cross entry no worse than four pence for over a year – mid-June 2009. The real clincher for the bulls came in the form of higher support above the 200 moving average from October onwards, after which with the 200 day line firmly in the ascent we had another confirmed super bull prospect. In fact there was plenty of time to get on the Hockey Stick express given the way that the shares were still well under 10p even as late as early October 2010.

As may be evident from just two examples, not only can picking penny stock minnows at literally the ground floor be a profitable exercise, it is a whole field (and new book) in itself. As a regular poster on the Sharecrazy.com community board I have access to the threads on companies where all the fundamentally hot stocks are discussed. It then does not take much to look at their charts and see which have the hockey stick move potential.

101 LESSONS LEARNT

From the perspective of someone making calls on the market on a daily basis, the process is all about advising/helping people survive in one of life's toughest arenas.

Imagining a critical audience, and having to produce extended and robust arguments and ideas almost means starting from scratch in terms of a charting approach. Whereas on Zaks-TA.com much time can be given to the subjective and even esoteric, in this book when faced with some of the most challenging events in the history of the financial markets I have been forced rather inadvertently to produce a trading system.

At least, the technical pillars of trading around chart gaps, the 200 day moving average, golden crosses (and if pushed RSI divergence), seem to be the most clear-cut ways of handling almost any situation. This discovery has certainly simplified even further my own approach to the markets, aware as I am that in volatile conditions having an extended checklist of criteria to wade through before clicking on the buy or sell button is simply not practical.

ABOUT THE AUTHOR

Saqib "Zak" Mir was born in Glasgow, Scotland to Pakistani immigrant Doctor parents in 1966. The family moved to London in the early 1970s and Zak attended prep school and then Harrow from 1980- 1984, which was distinguished only by winning the General Knowledge Prize in 1980. Successful A Level retakes following Harrow gave him the chance to be one of the few people in the world to fail interviews for Oxford (twice), Cambridge and Harvard, although he did subsequently get the chance turn down reading Theology at Oxford. There were then a few weeks at the LSE before the international airport (the run up to the Gaddafi era) atmosphere persuaded him to enter the City. From the early 1990s Zak was a derivatives broker at various companies such as Sucden, Union Cal (later part of Man Group) and Berkeley Futures.

From 2000 the opportunities afforded by the internet and the growth of Technical Analysis led to Zak being Shares Magazine's first Technical Editor, while in the meantime providing content to now defunct dot-coms such as TheStreet.co.uk and UKInvest.com.

In 2001 Zak teamed up with Tom "Show Me The Money" Winnifrith and his T1PS.com to found Zaks-TA.com, and provides white label research to some of the City of London's largest retail brokers via Brand Communications (Branduk.net).

Zak is now a Senior Analyst at the Institute of Trading and Portfolio Management (zakmir@instutrade.com).

He is the author of several books for ADVFN, and writes for their online newspaper. He also writes for a premium blog service on ADVFN, Zak Mir's AIM Stock Charting (www.advfn.com/newsletter/zakmir/).

Zak is married with three children and lives in Pamplona, Spain.

Follow Zak on Twitter: @zakmir

ALSO BY ZAK MIR

101 Charts for Trading Success

by Zak Mir

Using insider knowledge to reveal the tricks of the trade, Zak Mir's *101 Charts for Trading Success* explains the most complex set ups in the market. Illustrated with easy to understand charts this is the accessible, essential guide of how to read, understand and use charts to buy and sell stocks; a must for all future investment millionaires!

OTHER TITLES FROM ADVFN BOOKS

The Death of Wealth: The Economic Fall of the West

by Clem Chambers

Question: What is the next economic game changer?

Answer: The Death of Wealth.

Market guru Clem Chambers dissects the global economy and the state of the financial markets and the world's economies and lays out the evidence for the Death of Wealth.

ADVFN Guide:
The Beginner's Guide to Value Investing

by Clem Chambers

The stock market is not only for rich people, or those intent on gambling. 'Value Investing' is how Warren Buffet became the richest man in the world. A method of investing in the stock market without taking crazy risks, 'Value Investing' will help you build your fortune, no matter the economic climate. Perfect for novice investors, the book clearly outlines how to choose the best stocks and how – thanks to the Internet. It is the perfect way to ensure you 'get rich slow' with minimal stress.

ADVFN Guide:
101 Ways to Pick Stock Market Winners

by Clem Chambers

101 tips to help day traders, investors and stock pickers to focus on what characterises a potentially successful stock. Personally researched by Clem Chambers, one of the world's leading authorities on market performance. Incisive, brutally honest and occasionally very funny, *101 Ways to Pick Stock Market Winners* is an invaluable manual for anyone wanting to make money out of the markets.

Lessons From The Trader Wizard

by Bill Cara

New from trading legend and the Free Market Patriot Bill Cara, *Lessons From The Trader Wizard* teaches the tactics and skills to beat Wall Street. Bill shows you how to navigate the new world of trading the capital markets.

Evil's Good:
Book of Boasts and Other Investments

by Simon Cawkwell

Britain's most feared bear-raider spots overvalued stocks, shorts them and goes for the kill. He's been known to make £500,000 in a single week. In *Evil's Good* – part auto-biography, part financial training guide – Simon Cawkwell tells all of his market triumphs (and downfalls) and describes the 'shorting' rules that have made him so wealthy.

Go to www.advfnbooks.com for more information on these titles.

Printed in Great Britain
by Amazon

59538446R00113